THE LITTLE POCKET BOOK OF
MINDFULNESS

THE LITTLE POCKET BOOK OF
MINDFULNESS

Don't dwell on the past
or worry about the future

Simply BE in the present **WITH
MINDFULNESS MEDITATIONS**

ANNA BLACK

CICO BOOKS
LONDON NEW YORK

For Scott

Published in 2015 by CICO Books
An imprint of Ryland Peters & Small Ltd

20–21 Jockey's Fields   341 E 116th St
London WC1R 4BW   New York, NY 10029

www.rylandpeters.com

10 9 8 7 6

First published in 2012 as *Living In The Moment*

Text © Anna Black 2012
Design and illustration © CICO Books 2015

A CIP catalog record for this book
is available from the Library of Congress
and the British Library.

ISBN: 978 1 78249 203 0

Printed in China

Editor: Ingrid Court-Jones
Designer: Manisha Patel
Illustrator: Amy Louise Evans

In-house editor: Dawn Bates
In-house designer: Fahema Khanam
Art director: Sally Powell
Production: Mai-Ling Collyer
Publishing manager: Penny Craig
Publisher: Cindy Richards

CONTENTS

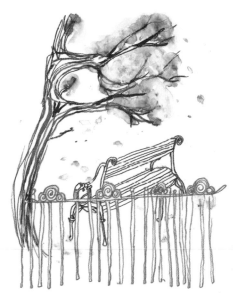

INTRODUCTION

Many of us operate on automatic pilot. How many times have you left the house and then later have no recollection of your actions since then—to the extent that you even might return to check you have actually shut or locked your front door? (And yes, I have done that!) To a certain extent we need to operate that way to get things done in the time we have available. But **problems arise when we spend the majority of our life in this way**—zoning out of the small, everyday experiences that add color and texture to life. Our lack of attention means we don't notice or we miss much that is going on and this affects our relationships. We multitask so much that we never stop to take stock of where we are—we are **constantly leaning forward to move on to the next thing**. Or we might be stuck; paralyzed with thoughts of "what if" or "if only" that prevent us moving forward and dealing with what is going on now. The negativity that arises out of these states of mind affects us even more and **we may become anxious or depressed, or we may self-medicate with drugs and alcohol**, and so the cycle continues. Very often the cycle is broken only by a major life change—an illness or an accident, a bereavement, a relationship breakdown. These are the type of events that jolt us awake and make us question the way we live. It is often **only when everything falls apart that we are prepared (and forced) to make radical changes.**

I discovered mindfulness by chance—browsing the local library's shelves I came across Jon Kabat-Zinn's book Full Catastrophe Living. Despite its thickness, the sub-title of "How to cope with stress, pain and illness using mindfulness meditation", sounded promising for someone who was struggling to cope with stress. Reading it was one of those "light bulb" moments as I realized how much energy I was expending trying to keep my life exactly how I thought it should be rather than accepting how it actually was. **The realization that I could stop struggling and start from where I actually was, gave me a huge feeling of release**—even though the acknowledgment of the size of the gap between reality and expectations was painful.

At the same time I was already interested in meditation, but I was not drawn to any traditional Buddhist orders. I was struggling with the practicalities—for example, in my yoga class the teacher would fold elegantly into the Lotus position and we would go into silence for 20 minutes. **I would close my eyes for what seemed an age only to open them and realize that the second hand of the clock had barely moved.** I would sit cross-legged, in agony, without a clue what I was supposed to be doing, and wonder how everyone else managed to sit there so serenely. One thing led to another, in the way it does if you let things unfold in their own time. I discovered there was no need to contort myself into an uncomfortable position; gradually, two minutes extended to five, then a few more, and so on.

Taking one step at a time (and a few backward), **I began to walk the path of mindfulness, keeping my attention firmly placed in my feet, while retaining an overall sense of the direction I was heading in.** My experience of each step encouraged and informed the next. Mindfulness now influences and guides my whole life. Its effects are not always easy to live with, and I often stumble and go off track, but connecting to one's own inner wisdom and strength takes you to a place of richness. We discover that we have to learn the same lessons over and over again— and that's okay—one never "arrives," but instead constantly learns and grows.

I have been influenced and taught so much by so many. Much of that is passed on here in the spirit of sharing that underpins Buddhist teachings, but any mistakes are mine. I hope this book will serve as a taster for **the possibilities that mindfulness meditation can bring into your own life** and encourage you to explore the subject further (see pages 204–7). The emphasis is on experimenting with ways to bring mindfulness into your everyday life, and doing this in small steps at a pace that feels right for you. You have a lifetime of moments filled with opportunity ahead of you.

chapter 1

WHAT IS MINDFULNESS?

Before trying any of the meditations in the book, it may help to have some understanding of what mindfulness is, where it comes from, and how it is being used today. Although its roots are over 2,500 years old, it is only in the last 30 years or so that it has been used therapeutically and become more mainstream. In this chapter I also **highlight the benefits of mindfulness** and explain how any one of us can draw out and cultivate these inherent qualities, as well as **dispel some common misconceptions about meditation.**

The book is designed for dipping in and out of, but before you begin practicing I recommend you read "How to Make the Most of this Book" on pages 15–19. This section has some important information about how to approach the practices and **get the most from them**, while always looking after yourself. To that end, there is also some guidance on posture and how to assume a position of alert attention that is safe and relaxed. Many of the meditations, though, can be done while you are out and about in daily life.

In mindfulness meditation we are deliberately cultivating particular attitudes that will support our practice and in this chapter I will explain what these are and **how they can benefit us—in everyday life** as well as in the practices themselves.

MINDFULNESS DEFINED

To begin with, it is helpful to have a clear understanding of what mindfulness is: **deliberately paying attention to things we normally would not even notice, and becoming aware of our present moment experience as it arises, non-judgmentally, and with kindness and compassion.** When we practice mindfulness, we pay attention to what is happening in our mind and our body; to our thoughts—the stories we tell ourselves—as well as to emotions and physical sensations as they are arising.

ORIGINS OF MINDFULNESS

Mindfulness meditation has its origins in Buddhist practices that are over 2,500 years old. Prince Siddhartha, who became the Buddha, dedicated his life to finding the cause of suffering and he recommended **mindfulness as a way of overcoming grief, sorrow, pain, and anxiety, and of realizing happiness.**

In 1979 **mindfulness began to be used therapeutically** by Dr Jon Kabat-Zinn and colleagues at the Stress Reduction Clinic at the University of Massachusetts Hospital, USA. Kabat-Zinn developed the eight-week Mindfulness-Based Stress Reduction (MBSR) program as a way of helping people learn to live with chronic medical conditions. These were people who the doctors could do nothing more for—for example, those with terminal illness, chronic back pain, or who had HIV. Many of them were suffering from depression and anxiety as a result of their condition.

In MBSR, mindfulness is cultivated through formal meditation practices, such as sitting and the body scan, as well as mindful movement, such as yoga, and informal practices in which participants bring mindfulness meditation into their everyday lives. Through these practices **participants discover a different way of being with their suffering**. The program cultivates qualities such as patience, acceptance, and equanimity, which enable them to deal with stress, chronic pain, and illness with greater ease, skill, and wisdom. Clinical research has shown that **beneficial physical changes occur** in participants completing the course, including a stronger immune system, lower blood pressure, and shifts in the way the brain deals with difficult emotions. The benefits of the MBSR program spread by word of mouth and through the media, and it was soon offered to people of all ages in all walks of life. Today, MBSR programs are popular in schools, prisons, and in the sports and business worlds, as well as in healthcare, where they are **practiced as much by healthcare providers as by patients themselves.**

In 2001 Mindfulness-Based Cognitive Therapy (MBCT) was developed by Mark Williams, John Teasdale, and Zindel V. Segal. Based on MBSR, MBCT was developed specifically for the treatment of depression, but has since been adapted for other clinical conditions, including anxiety, eating disorders, and addictions. MBCT is recommended by NICE (the National Institute for Health and

Clinical Excellence) in the UK for the treatment of depression in individuals who have suffered three or more episodes.

In essence MBSR and MBCT are very similar. There is a difference in that MBSR is usually taught to generic groups of people suffering from a variety of physical and psychological conditions or disorders and/or general life stress, whereas MBCT is usually taught to a group suffering from a specific condition, such as depression or anxiety, and so would include course content appropriate for that condition. However, the **emphasis on the deliberate and non-judgmental present-moment awareness of one's own experience is at the core** of both MBSR and MBCT.

The evidence base for the therapeutic uses of mindfulness-based approaches to health is growing all the time. Research is commonly done with participants on a structured eight-week course, incorporating a daily practice of both formal and informal meditations, as well as classroom teaching. The practices in this book are predominantly informal and, although they are not a substitute for therapeutic care, they are a good place to start practicing mindfulness if you are a beginner.

If you already have some experience of mindfulness meditation, I hope this book will encourage you to bring it more into your daily life. While the formal practices are without doubt important, the more we can weave mindfulness into the fabric of our lives, the more we will reap the benefits.

HOW TO MAKE THE MOST OF THIS BOOK

The book has been divided into different chapters. If you are new to mindfulness, I recommend you start with some of the body-focused practices in Chapter 2, Tuning in to the Body. These will **introduce some core skills, such as breath awareness and moving the attention around the body,** which are needed for practices in which we learn to "be with the difficult," such as pain or anxiety. It is always best to **take small steps rather than jump in at the deep end.** Chapter 5, Weaving Your Parachute, has some foundational practices that underpin and cultivate attitudes and skills, which will help you get the most out of all the meditations. Once you are used to focusing on the breath, it is fine to dip in and out of the different sections.

A key component of mindfulness is the **willingness to turn toward the difficult**—uncomfortable sensations in the body, painful emotions, or unwanted thoughts. As our awareness increases we notice much that previously we have tuned out from because it was unpleasant or painful, either physically or psychologically. Paying **attention to the body can also**

bring old emotions to the surface. All of this means that, while mindfulness meditation can have many benefits, it can also be stressful and, at times, difficult. If at any time you feel overwhelmed, it is important that you stop immediately. It does not mean that you will never be able to practice mindfulness, but perhaps it might be better to do it with the support of a teacher or at a time when things are less stressful for you. If in doubt, always seek the advice of your doctor.

I recommend that you take the time to read through the following guidance before embarking on any of the practices. When you come to do a practice, I suggest you read it through a few times and then set aside the book and have a go. **There is never just one way to do something and the instructions are for guidance only.** The more you do the practices the more you will make them your own, using your own words, phrases, and rhythms that will have a particular resonance for you. Feel free also to make practices longer or shorter as you wish. Many of them can be extended to whatever time you have available.

The more you do the practices the more you will make

REMEMBER

✳ Mindfulness is about deliberately paying attention to your experience, without judgment, as it unfolds—noticing what is happening physically in the body and where. It also involves being aware of what emotions are arising and the tone of these feelings, as well as noticing the stories we tell ourselves.

✳ The emphasis is always on *what* is happening, not *why* it is happening.

✳ We use our senses—sight, sound, taste, touch, and smell—to explore our experience.

✳ We never look for a particular experience. There is no right or wrong experience. Whatever your experience is, this is your experience in this moment.

✳ If at any time you get lost in a practice, just bring your attention back to the physical sensations of breathing.

them your own, using your own words, phrases, and rhythms

QUESTIONS YOU MIGHT ASK YOURSELF WHILE PRACTICING ARE:

∗ What am I feeling physically in my body? Notice what the sensation is, where it is located and its particular characteristic—for example, whether it is constant or changing, and so on.

∗ What am I feeling emotionally? If you identify a particular emotion—for example, anger—ask yourself: How do I know I am feeling angry? Where am I experiencing anger in my body? What do the physical sensations of anger feel like? How would I describe them?

∗ What thoughts are arising? What stories am I telling myself about my experience?

You can do many of the practices while you are out and about in your daily life—standing in lines, or sitting in your car or a waiting room. But **for others you will need to find a quiet place where you won't be disturbed.** I have known students who retire to the bathroom at work in order to have a few minutes undisturbed meditation time!

Wherever you are, I suggest you **turn off or unplug your phone**. If you are worried about finishing at a particular time, I would recommend setting your phone to vibrate or using a timer or alarm clock, but perhaps put it under a cushion or a pillow so that the sudden ringing does not startle you too much. There is some guidance about posture on pages 38–41.

Some people find keeping a meditation journal helpful so that they can record their experiences, and nowadays there are even phone apps that allow you to do this.

It is easy for your mindfulness practice to be relegated to yet another item on your list of things to do, so I suggest you **keep it simple and perhaps focus on just one practice to start with**. It's best to do one practice several times a week, or whenever you remember, before experimenting with something new. Congratulate yourself on what you do manage to do rather than berate yourself for what you don't accomplish.

HOW CAN MINDFULNESS HELP US?

The body has a built-in alarm system, which is called the "stress reaction" and it also has a corresponding "calming response." This alarm system, known as the "fight-or-flight" mechanism, has ensured our evolutionary survival, but nowadays too often it is triggered repeatedly by everyday stresses rather than the life or death situations of our ancestors. However, **mindfulness can help to switch off the stress reaction and to activate the calming response**.

We all suffer from stress, so it is useful to have some understanding of what stress is and the role it plays in our lives. It is a complex subject and the following explanation has been greatly simplified, but there are plenty of books in which you can read about the stress response in more detail (see pages 204–7). The human body is hot-wired for stress. **The effectiveness of our stress reaction has ensured our survival and consequently our default setting is one of hyper vigilance**. The "enemies" we face today may be different from those our hunter-gatherer ancestors encountered, but the way in which we process danger remains the same. In fact, the fight-or-flight mechanism is operated by the amygdala, one of the most primitive parts of our brain.

The brain is constantly processing information received through our senses. If something or someone is perceived as a threat, the body's alarm system is activated instantly, preparing it to fight or flee by diverting all the body's resources to deal with the emergency.

* Energy, as epinephrine (adrenaline), is released – as well as other stress hormones that activate the body's emergency systems – to help you run faster or fight the danger.
* The heart speeds up, beating three or four times faster than usual to pump blood around the body as quickly as possible, so that the arms and legs can function optimally to fight or run.
* Long-term bodily functions, such as growth, digestion, and the reproductive system, are shut down—the rationale being that if you are killed by the threat, you won't need to grow, digest your food, or reproduce.
* The body evacuates any waste matter, which is extra weight, so that it is as light as possible to flee. This is why we may feel the need to visit the bathroom when we are stressed.

You may notice how your skin goes clammy in stressful moments. This is because blood is being pulled away from the body's surface to support the heart and muscles, and to reduce blood loss in case of injury. You also feel butterflies in the stomach as the digestive system is shutting down, and your heart begins beating rapidly as it pumps faster. In addition, your pupils dilate so that you can see better; the scalp tightens and your hair seems to stand on end (your body hair does this, too) so that you can sense danger through vibrations; your mouth goes dry because fluid is being diverted from nonessential locations; and in some people, the throat goes into spasm.

Simultaneously, while the body is activated for action, the brain continues to gather information from the senses about the alleged threat, as well as from the higher centers of the brain, accessing memories and comparing the threat against any previous, similar experiences, including those we may have experienced second-hand. What the brain discovers determines whether it deactivates or maintains the alert. If we respond negatively to what we are experiencing, the brain will determine that something bad is happening to us and keep the body on alert. Therefore, although **our thoughts and our memories have an important role to play in safeguarding us from danger**, they can also work against us and perpetuate an unfounded threat.

When the fight-or-flight mechanism is repeatedly and needlessly activated through everyday stress, the consequences can be serious and our long-term body systems can become vulnerable to disease. The constant increase in blood pressure heightens our risk of heart disease; the stress hormones affect insulin activity and thereby increase the risk of diabetes; our immune system can be compromised; and our memory and our thought processes are disrupted, so we operate less efficiently. The presence of the stress hormone cortisol can cause long-term damage by overactivating the amygdala, thereby promoting fear and negativity. It also reduces neural branching and inhibits the growth of new neurons, so **we remain stuck in old, fearful beliefs**. The mood we are in affects our interpretation of events—a low mood is more likely to produce a negative interpretation of a neutral event. Excessive cortisol also causes the area of the brain that produces new brain cells to wither and die. Chronic **stress strengthens the negative networks in the brain** and weakens the positive ones.

We often cope with these unpleasant reactions to stress by artificial means, such as consuming alcohol, taking medication, or working harder, which only compound and perpetuate the cycle.

Surprisingly, perhaps, the **small everyday stresses are more harmful to us in the long term** than one-off, hugely stressful events. And the more often the stress reaction is activated, the more likely it is be triggered again, giving the body less and less time to recover. In this way, we become stuck in a never-ending cycle.

Once the stress reaction has been activated, **the natural way to remove the stress hormones from the body is through action**—for our ancestors this meant fighting or running away. Obviously, physically fighting or **running away are rarely options in our everyday lives**, but any exercise, such as walking vigorously, running, or swimming, can achieve the same results and bring the body back to a state of equilibrium. Unfortunately, we cannot always take exercise at the moment of feeling stressed.

However, **we can activate the calming response through mindfulness and we can do this anywhere**. If we can intervene at the point where the brain is gathering further information about the perceived threat, we can respond rather than react, as we can contextualize and interpret the situation more wisely. We can see the threat for what it really is—and if it is a false alarm, the stress reaction is deactivated. We can do this by **noticing what is happening to us**, paying attention to the uncomfortable physical sensations, and thereby shifting from thinking about the threat and all of the possible consequences to simply experiencing it as it unfolds. Mindfulness **breaks the cycle of rumination**, which keeps the amygdala in the alert position.

Practicing mindfulness de-sensitizes the stress trigger and thereby allows the body to return to a state of equilibrium rather than remain hyper vigilant. **People who practice mindfulness still experience stress, and may actually feel emotions more strongly, but they are less likely to be overcome by it** and they are likely to recover more quickly.

How stressful an event is for us depends on how we perceive it. If we can change the way we perceive an event, we can change our response to it. So mindfulness can **activate the body's built-in calming response**. It can also help us in other ways.

Research after the eight-week MBSR course has shown that physical changes occur in the body: blood pressure can be reduced, the immune system strengthened, and the brain can even change the way it processes information. A study by Richard Davidson and colleagues discovered that after an MBSR course, participants showed a marked shift in brain activation toward the area better able to handle difficult emotions. It had been previously believed this was a set point in each individual that was more or less fixed for life, but Davidson's research showed that we **can actually influence and change our brain to make it work for the better**.

There are also psychological benefits. **Most of us spend the majority of time in our heads rather than our bodies**. We problem-solve our way through life and while that can be effective in the office or when running our home, we cannot treat our emotions in the same way. When we try to do so, we become caught in a spin-cycle of thinking, replaying events over and over in our mind in a way that is unhelpful and can spiral into anxiety and depression.

At the same time, **we are often unaware of what is going on in the body**. Either we are uninterested or we deliberately block out unpleasant sensations and emotions. Sometimes numbing out physical or emotional pain can be an important coping strategy, but we often continue using it long after the threat has passed. Our body can give us essential feedback on what we are feeling emotionally and physically. By **becoming more attuned to our body, we become more informed about how a particular event or situation is affecting us** and we are also more likely to pick up early warning signs of physical and psychological illness.

When we practice mindfulness, we are deliberately **turning our attention to our thoughts, our emotions, and physical sensations as they are arising**. We begin to notice habitual patterns of thinking or behavior. We become aware of the constraints and boxes we create around ourselves. We often realize how mindless we are and how much of our life is passing us by unnoticed as we are caught up in re-living the past or waiting for a better future. However, as Jon Kabat-Zinn says, **the present moment is** the only moment **where it is possible to change**. And we can only make wise changes if we are truly aware of what our experience really is. The moment of awareness that is cultivated through mindfulness offers a window of opportunity **to respond differently**. It creates a space that can be enough to make us think twice about our habitual reaction. That small shift can be enough to turn us in a very different direction and we are more likely to **respond with greater wisdom**.

There is a growing evidence base for the clinical benefits of MBSR and MBCT, but there are benefits for all of us, regardless of whether we are suffering physical or emotional pain. Suffering is a part of life. We are all going to experience grief, loss, and death at some point and many of us will experience illness and other traumatic life events. Even happy events, such as a wedding or the birth of a child, can be stressful. However, **much of the daily stress we experience that has a negative effect on our health, well-being, and personal relationships is made up of repeated occurrences of small events**: missing a train, forgetting an appointment, losing work on the computer, saying something hurtful to a loved one, and so on.

If we start to **pay attention to the moments that make up every day**, we can begin to do things differently, and moment by moment, step by step, we can change our life for the better. When we wake up to the moments in life, we experience what Kabat-Zinn calls "the full catastrophe" of life: the joyful, the difficult, the painful, the boring. We begin to notice how **life is in constant flux**—just like the weather—and **the possibility of change is always present**. We realize that all human beings suffer and that life is often difficult. Everyone else is not always happy and living an idyllic, perfect life, despite what the media might lead us to believe.

Realizing that we are not failures just because we are experiencing unhappiness can be liberating.

When we do formal meditation practices, such as a sitting meditation, all the difficult emotions we experience in daily life—boredom, restlessness, impatience, irritation, fear, and anger—will appear at some point, as well as the positive ones. The **formal practices offer an opportunity to practice being with difficult emotions in a place of relative safety**, thereby allowing us to deal with them more effectively when we experience them in daily life.

As we become aware of our thoughts, we begin to realize how **much of our own unhappiness is caused by the stories we tell ourselves**. For example, say you stub your toe on a bag that has been left on the floor by your partner. You experience the physical pain of the toe making contact with the bag. This is the first dart. Then, if you are like the majority of us, you begin ranting about the bag

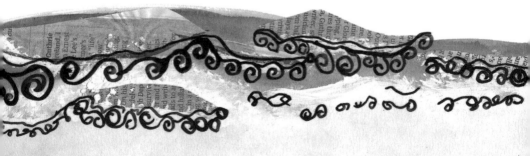

being left on the floor and before you know it you are accusing your partner of not loving or respecting you, or berating yourself for not doing better at school/having a better job/being able to afford a bigger house, and so on. You may even wonder if the toe is broken and what the consequences of that might be. These stories are the second dart. We cannot do anything about the first dart, because this is physical suffering. However, we can do something about the second dart; we can **become aware of the stories and let them go**. This part is within our control.

Learning to let go is not easy. When we practice watching the breath (or indeed any point of focus, such as a sound or a sensation), we gently escort our attention back to the breath every time our mind wanders. We are practicing letting go of that thought. We do this over and over again every time we practice and in doing so, we practice letting go.

REMEMBER

We practice. Practicing entails repetition. Practicing takes time and effort. Mindfulness is not a quick fix. To truly experience transformational change, you need to **make mindfulness an integral part of your life**. Although this might sound daunting, remind yourself that **all change occurs through small steps** and by reading this book you have already taken the first one. Just as stress arises through small events that we perceive as stressful, we can **begin to undo the negative effects with small actions.**

WHO CAN PRACTICE MINDFULNESS?

While mindfulness is a trait that is naturally stronger in some people than others, this also means that it is something inherent in all of us, which can be cultivated, strengthened, and drawn out. Mindfulness can be of benefit to anyone, but the following people may find it particularly helpful:

* Those who are carers or in the caring professions. When we are looking after others, it can be very difficult to make time for ourselves. However, our primary responsibility should be to ourselves—then we will be better able to look after others.

* Those who have a history of repeated bouts of depression, rather than one episode of depression in response to a single life event. Mindfulness may not prevent a future relapse, but hopefully it will help you spot the warning signs of depression sooner and so the relapse will be shorter and less severe.

* Those who suffer from anxiety. We become anxious when we dwell on the past or worry about the future. The "what ifs" and "if onlys" can tie us up in knots. In mindfulness, the

emphasis on the present moment can stop the downward spiral, and focusing on the sensations you feel in your body can help pull you out of the negative mindset.

∗ Those who suffer from a chronic illness or condition. Mindfulness can help us learn to live with illness rather than be consumed by it. By noticing the moment-to-moment changes in the mind and body we are better able to make use of those times, and also to recognize when it is better to rest and recuperate.

∗ Those who suffer from chronic or intermittent pain. We increase our suffering with the stories we tell ourselves about pain; and we tense the body to withstand and resist pain and, in doing so, create additional stress and tension elsewhere. Mindfulness can help us move up close to the pain so that we become more familiar with its characteristics and notice the stories we tell ourselves, which enables us to become less caught up in it. Pain is present, but we are much more than the pain.

∗ Those who feel stressed or overwhelmed. Mindfulness can help deactivate the stress reaction (see page 20).

∗ Those who are going through a period of change in their life. Participants often come to the course when something has changed in their life, perhaps children have left home, or they have been made redundant, or a relationship has come to an end. The seemingly solid ground of their day-to-day life has shifted.

∗ Those who realize they would like something to be different in their life, even if they are not sure what. These people have not been formally diagnosed with anything specific.

Practicing mindfulness is about rebalancing our lives, and we can all get something different from it. People who are very loud and gregarious may learn to temper their responses in public and learn to listen to others. The shy mouse may learn to speak out and be heard. Another person may lose weight because he or she starts noticing an automatic impulse to eat when feeling down. A by-product for me was that I began to recycle my household waste—before practicing mindfulness I had thought there was little point because my small contribution could not make any difference in the overall scheme of things. **When we practice mindfulness we realize the smallest things do make a difference and every thought and action has a consequence.** We can influence what happens next by making deliberate choices about how we respond in the present moment. This has implications on every level of life from the personal to the global.

Beginners often think their mind is too busy for meditation. A common Buddhist analogy is to talk of the "monkey mind" with thoughts jumping from subject to subject like monkeys from tree to tree. If we wish to, **any one of us can learn to meditate.** The variety of meditation practices allows room to experiment—for example, people sometimes find mindful movement helpful and easier than sitting practice when their mind is particularly restless.

There are many different forms of meditation practice: some focus solely on developing concentration, others use props, such as candles or music, as a point of focus. Other meditation practices, such as Tai chi, Qi Gong, and yoga, involve movement and there are even dance/meditation practices. Mindfulness is practiced by many Buddhist orders and forms part of many Buddhist traditions. **The various** traditions and methods are often just different doorways into the same room, so experiment to find out what appeals to you.

It is possible to practice mindfulness meditation at any age. Young children are naturally more mindful than adults as they very much live in the present moment, but author and educator Susan Kaiser Greenland is teaching forms of mindfulness to children as young as four. Teenagers can find it particularly helpful. However, **choice is an integral part of mindfulness** and it is counter-productive to direct or try to force anyone to practice.

It is never too late to begin practicing mindfulness and if your practice lapses, you can always begin again.

> *It is important to realize that the mind will always wander. I find it reassuring to hear meditation teachers who have practiced for over forty years talk of their wandering mind! It is what minds do. When our mind wanders, we notice where it has gone and then gently and kindly bring our attention back to the point of focus (the breath, the sound, or whatever is being used as a focus.) We do this once, twice, ten thousand times—and that is the practice. Every time our mind wanders we have an opportunity to practice letting go and coming back; Jon Kabat-Zinn likens it to working out in the gym, but instead we are exercising the muscle of awareness.*

COMMON MISCONCEPTIONS

People often have concerns about meditation or perhaps have half heard about different techniques, so it is helpful to clarify some common misconceptions.

We are not trying to empty or clear our mind when we meditate; instead **we are observing our thoughts and noticing common patterns or stories**. Generally, we are unaware of the stories that are influencing and driving all our actions and decisions. By **bringing them into awareness, we are in a better position to discard those that are unhelpful** and deliberately encourage those that are helpful.

We do not need to sit in the Lotus position to meditate. **It is not the position that is important, but the attitude of mind we bring to it**. If you suffer from a physical condition that means you would find it difficult to do a practice as suggested, such as lying on the floor, then it is always fine to adapt and change it to suit how you are at this moment. See pages 38–41 for more guidance on posture.

There is no conflict with any religion or religious beliefs. Many religions practice forms of meditation. The practices described in this book are completely secular, although they may have their roots in Buddhist practices.

We are not meditating in order to relax or, indeed, to achieve any particular state of mind. We may become more relaxed as a result of meditating, but if we set out to become relaxed by meditating we are setting ourselves up for failure and disappointment. When we meditate we are opening ourselves to whatever arises. All mind states and emotions will arise at some point—particularly when we do formal practices—and this presents us with opportunities to be with difficult emotions in a safe environment. In this way **we can cultivate skills that we can then put into practice when difficult emotions arise in everyday life**.

Mindfulness is not positive thinking. We are not trying to convince ourselves that everything in the world is wonderful. On the contrary, **mindfulness is about opening to all experience: the good, the bad, and the neutral**. Each is as worthy of our attention as the others. We need to acknowledge and experience the dark as well as the light, and all of the shades of gray in between. Through opening up to the full spectrum we begin to see how circumstances change and states of mind ebb and flow like the tide, and that nothing is fixed forever. **There always exists the possibility for change, however small**.

Mindfulness is definitely not a quick fix or a miracle cure. **Practicing mindfulness meditation requires a commitment and a willingness to be with whatever arises**, and this can be challenging.

When we talk of "living in the moment," this does not mean living without any thought to the future. **Living in the moment simply means paying attention to our experience as it happens**. By knowing (and acknowledging) what is actually happening in this moment we are better able to take care of and influence what is going to happen next.

HELPFUL ATTITUDES

Meditation is an active process and **if you want to bring about change in your life, it requires a deliberate engagement on your part**. No one else can do this for you and how you approach it is important. In *Full Catastrophe Living*, Jon Kabat-Zinn stresses the importance of particular attitudes that are helpful to cultivate and form the bedrock upon which our mindfulness practice rests.

THE FOLLOWING ARE PARTICULARLY HELPFUL ATTITUDES TO BRING TO MIND WHEN YOU ARE DOING ANY OF THE PRACTICES IN THIS BOOK:

CURIOSITY One of the joys of spending time with a child is seeing the world through his or her eyes, where everything is new and interesting. Too often we see our world through a scratched and cloudy filter of experience, which means we see only half the picture and it is often distorted or obscured. When we pay attention to our experience with the curiosity of a child, seeing it as if for the very first time, all kinds of possibilities take shape.

NOT STRIVING One of the paradoxes of meditation is that if we do it with a specific expectation in mind, we are setting ourselves up for disappointment. As soon as we set ourselves a goal, we find ourselves measuring constantly to see how near or how far we are from achieving it. It is more helpful to remind ourselves that the easiest way to get from A to B is simply to focus on being here, at A.

TRUST Learning to trust the process and letting it unfold is important. As you begin to tune in to the body and pay attention to the feedback you find there, you will access your inner wisdom. **Trust in yourself and your intuition; if something does not feel right for you, do not do it.**

PATIENCE Mindfulness is not a quick fix. You may not feel or see a difference for a while and it takes time to unlearn the habits of a lifetime. There is no rush and the learning is in the journey.

NOT JUDGING When we begin to pay attention to our thoughts, the first thing we often notice is how judgmental we are—toward others and ourselves. Our judgments color all our interactions and we often practice a degree of meanness and even hatred toward ourselves that goes far beyond how we would dream of treating someone else. However, it is just as unhelpful to criticize our judging mind and so, instead, we notice and acknowledge it with compassion and come back to the point of focus. Practicing kindness is as important as practicing mindfulness—mindfulness without kindness is not mindfulness.

ACCEPTANCE This does not mean passive resignation, but instead **seeing things how they really are, rather than how we would like them to be**.

LETTING GO This means releasing the need to fix or change things to how you want them to be. **Allowing things to be as they are is a form of acceptance**.

It is helpful, too, to remind yourself that you don't have to enjoy it! Mindfulness can make our experiences richer and more vivid, but greater self-awareness can also make us become more aware of difficulties in our lives.. Letting ourselves off the hook in terms of enjoying our practice can make a difference.

It also can be useful to view your practice as an experiment, with you as the subject. Bring an attitude of curiosity to it—what do you notice if you do this or if you do that? **Your practice is a process of discovery and exploration rather than one of judgment and evaluation**.

POSTURE

None of the practices in this book require pretzel-like contortions of the body. When doing a sitting practice you can sit either on an upright kitchen or dining chair, or on the floor. You may experience pins and needles or some minor discomfort while sitting and this provides **an opportunity to practice being with uncomfortable sensations**, but you certainly do not want to be sitting with any pain. Therefore do **experiment with different positions and props**. You can even do a "sitting" practice lying flat on your back if that feels more appropriate for you. The most important thing when meditating is that you **listen to your body and**

make any adjustments needed to the suggested posture. The attitude you bring to a sitting practice is more important than the posture itself.

SITTING ON A CHAIR

Sit on an upright kitchen or dining chair, then bend over and, while touching your toes (or reaching down as far as you are able), wriggle your buttocks to the back of the chair and then sit up. You will now be sitting in an upright, yet unsupported, position. **If you feel it is necessary, you can place a small cushion behind your lower back, but you want to avoid slumping back into the seat.** Both feet should be firmly planted on the floor—you can place a cushion underneath the feet for support. It can be helpful to raise the back legs of the chair 1 in (2.5cm) or so off the ground with small blocks of wood or a book. This helps tilt the pelvis correctly.

SITTING ON THE FLOOR

You can sit cross-legged or kneel on the floor. Either way **your hips should always be higher than your knees**, so you may need to sit on several cushions or large books to achieve this. If your knees do not touch the floor, you may want to support them with cushions, folded up blankets, or pillows.

If you prefer a kneeling position, sit back on your heels and support the buttocks with a cushion or a meditation bench. Do **experiment, as the height of your support can make a big difference.** When you have the right height and position, you will feel comfortable and balanced.

Whether you are sitting on a chair, a stool, or on the floor, **the lower limbs should be grounded and supported.** The upper part of the body should rise out of the waist—it can be helpful to imagine a silken thread running up from the base of the spine, through the back, the neck, and out of the back of the head. If this thread was pulled, your torso would gently rise out of the waist and your chin tuck in slightly. We are looking for **a posture that is alert and upright, yet relaxed.**

Your hands should be relaxed and supported—you can clasp them in your lap lightly, or rest them with your palms face down or up, on your knees. Your eyes can be open or closed; if they are open, perhaps look ahead and down with a soft unfocused gaze. Closing your eyes can be a way of sinking deeper into your practice, but experiment and explore the differences yourself.

STANDING

You can do many of the informal practices in this book while you are out and about. While **there is no need to take an obvious meditation stance,** it can be helpful to bring yourself into a balanced, stable position.

So, for example, rather than lounging against the bus stop, stand with your weight evenly spread across both feet.

BECOMING AWARE

Our internal state of mind often reflects our external posture; so if your body is slumped and caving in, your mind will often feel contracted and tight. Turn your attention to your sitting position. How are you sitting? How do you feel emotionally? Experiment with adjusting your posture and noticing any changes.

HOUSEHOLD OBJECTS TO SUPPORT YOUR PRACTICE:

When sitting on the floor, use a cushion or pillow either to lift your buttocks so they are higher than your hips or to support your knees. The cushion(s) should be as firm as possible. You may need several for sufficient height. If you start sitting on the floor regularly, you may want to invest in a meditation cushion (a zafu) or a bench.

Stack a few books on top of each other if you need extra height on a meditation bench, or sitting on the floor, or for supporting the feet if you are sitting on a chair.

A yoga mat, a towel, or a blanket are useful when you are lying on the floor. The body's temperature can drop quite markedly when you are still, so it is helpful to have a blanket or a shawl to hand when practicing, in case you feel cold.

chapter 2

TUNING IN TO THE BODY

Most of us spend more time in our heads than in our bodies. Unfortunately, **we cannot think our way out of emotional upsets, and trying to do so can actually make us feel worse**. The practices in this section will help redress this imbalance.

By regularly tuning in to the body we can gain valuable feedback in terms of our emotional and physical well-being. These practices will help develop concentration and provide an opportunity to practice directing the breath into different parts of the body. The **emphasis on the breath will enable you to begin to use it as an anchor**. Whenever your mind wanders (and it will), you can use the breath to reel yourself back into the body and the present moment.

Deliberately turning toward something we habitually avoid can release strong emotions, so if at any point you feel overwhelmed during any of the practices, please just take a break and stop. You can return to it another time. We are learning to **trust our own inner wisdom and listen to the body**, therefore if at any time any instruction does not feel appropriate for you, simply refrain from doing it. There is always an "edge" around sitting with discomfort, such as an itch, but at no point should you tolerate pain—if necessary, adjust your position, and **always follow any medical advice you have been given.**

MINDFULNESS
OF BREATHING

Focusing on the breath is a great place to start if you are new to meditation. The instruction is simple: pay attention to the breath.

Experiment with tuning in to the breath at odd times during the day when you remember (no one else will know you are doing it.) If you would like to start practicing more formally, set aside five minutes to sit quietly somewhere and pay attention to the breath. Gradually extend the length of time, but remember **the quality of attention is more important than the length of time you sit**.

There are more breath-focused meditations on pages 146–51.

the quality of attention is more important than the length of time you sit

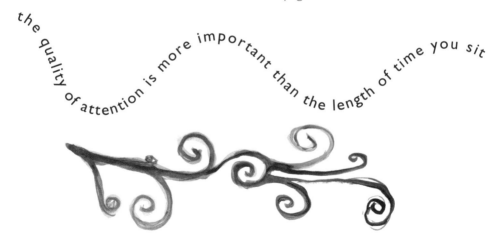

Try this

It can be helpful to choose an area of the body in which you feel the breath most strongly—for example in the belly, the chest, around the nostrils or the lips, and always take your attention to this place when doing a breathing practice. If you find it difficult to locate a place, perhaps place a hand on your belly or on your chest, so you can feel the act of breathing.

Then, just notice the sensations of breathing—this is different from thinking about the breath. What we are doing here is feeling the expansion as the chest and the belly rise on the in-breath… and noticing the contraction as the chest and the belly fall on the out-breath.

REMEMBER

We are staying with the length of each in-breath, then the length of each out-breath. Whenever our mind wanders (which it will), gently escort it back to the breath and continue.

CLEANSING THE BODY
WITH BREATH

This simple practice is a form of body scan. The easiest way to do it is lying down, but you could also do it sitting or reclining. Here you are **learning to focus on and direct the breath into and around the body,** as well as deliberately tuning in to a wider awareness of your body.

Try this

Take your attention to the breath and focus on the part of your body where you feel it most strongly — perhaps the belly, or the chest or around the lips and nostrils... and stay with your experience of the breath... breathing in... and breathing out... feeling the sensations of breathing... allowing the breath to breathe itself... letting go of any need to direct or manipulate the breath in any way... breathing in... and breathing out... supported and held by the surface you are lying on... resting with the breath... breathing in ... and breathing out...

Now, taking your attention to the breath, imagine it is sweeping through the body... breathing in through the crown of the head... filling the body with breath... and breathing out through the soles of the feet...

Then, breathing in through the soles of the feet... allowing the body to fill with breath... with life... with energy... and breathing out through the crown of the head...

Continue in this way, sweeping the body with breath, breathing in and breathing out from top to bottom.

THE HAND

In this practice we are paying attention to the hand—the part of the body that caresses, touches, grabs, and so on—and **reflecting on what it does for us moment by moment, day after day, year after year.**

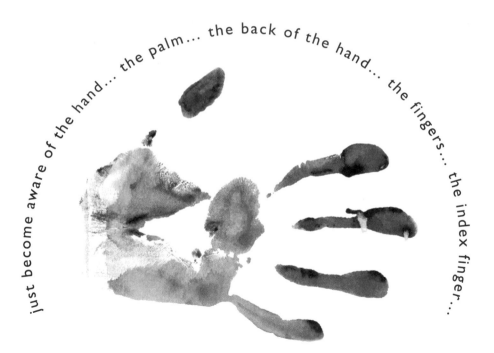

just become aware of the hand... the palm... the back of the hand... the fingers... the index finger...

Try this

Take your attention to one of your hands. In your mind's eye, just become aware of the hand... the palm... the back of the hand... the fingers... the index finger... the middle finger... the ring finger... the little finger... the thumb. Becoming aware of the length of each finger... notice the spaces in between... in your mind's eye becoming aware of the thumb nail... and then the other nails.

We are not looking for any particular sensations and you may have none at all—if so, that is your experience now.

Slowly move one of your fingers. Experiment with slowly stretching and bending the finger, feeling the stretch... noticing the contraction...

What is it like if you bring a finger and thumb together? What sensations are you noticing? Gently rub the finger and thumb back and forth together... moving them apart and bringing them together... becoming aware of any sensations of touch. Play with moving... adjusting, bending, stretching the different fingers on the hand. Moving them singly, moving them together...

Next, expand your awareness to the whole hand. Begin rotating your hand at the wrist... first one way and then the other... turning... noticing the limit of the turn... and then coming back... repeating the movement.

What you do today may be different from what you did yesterday or what you may do tomorrow. We are simply interested in the hand in this moment—what it can do, what it feels like.

THE FACE

It is best to do this practice at home or somewhere private where you won't be disturbed. You can do it sitting up or lying down. The purpose is to **practice tuning in to the body**, moving your attention and breath around a particular area.

Try this

Closing your eyes (if that feels okay to you), taking your attention to your face… just become aware of the face… perhaps exploring its boundaries… where it begins and ends…

Then begin focusing your attention on specific parts of the face… the jaw… the lips… the mouth… inside the mouth… the tongue… the teeth… the nose… Notice the eyes… the eyeballs resting in the sockets of the skull… protected by the eyelids… feeling the weight of the eyes resting here…

Now focus on the forehead and the temples… the ears… the left ear… the right ear… the scalp… in your mind's eye, massaging the scalp with awareness.

All the time keep an active interest and curiosity about this face and these features… this face exactly as it is right now… letting go of any need or wish to assume a particular expression or pose… just allowing the face to be here as it is… Notice if any judgments arise and if they do, perhaps just noting "judging is here," before bringing your attention back to the face with kindness and gentleness.

Simply be with your experience, whatever it may be.

SETTLING IN TO THE BODY

I came across this practice in a book called *Emotional Healing through Mindfulness Meditation* by psychotherapist Barbara Miller Fishman, but it is also part of a Yoga Nidra (a body scan that helps to achieve a deep-sleep state in yoga.) It is a short practice that is best done lying down. I find it **a particularly quick way to get into the body** if I am lying awake with a racing mind. In this body scan we move around the body in sections.

I find it is helpful to have a visual picture in my head of an outstretched body and to **imagine it being segmented into the different parts** (I always picture a magician cutting his assistant in half!) I usually do this practice lying down because it is harder for me to visualize when I am in a sitting position, but experiment for yourself and see. The order does not matter and you can always **leave out sections if you wish to shorten the exercise** or repeat it a couple of times if you prefer a longer practice.

Try this

Lying down with your feet stretched out and falling away from each other, and your arms down by your sides... your eyes closed if that feels comfortable for you... become aware of the right side of the body... from the right side of the top of the head to the tip of the right foot... including the right arm... Just become aware of the right side of the body, staying with this for a few moments.

Now, leaving the right side of the body, become aware of the left side of the body... the whole of the left side of the body from the top of the head right down to the tip of the left foot... holding the left side of the body in awareness... staying with this for a few moments.

Next, become aware of the top half of the body... noticing the torso from the waist upward and through to the top of the head... including both the left and right arms... holding the top half of the body in awareness... staying with this for a few moments.

Then, leaving the top half of the body, take your attention to the lower half of the body... becoming aware of the area below the waist... including both the left and right legs... just holding the lower half of the body in awareness... staying with this for a few moments.

Now, become aware of the front of the body—so in your mind's eye you are picturing the front of the body... the face... the chest... the front of the arms... the belly... the front of the thighs... the knees... the shins... the front of the feet... holding the entire front of the body in awareness... staying with this for a few moments.

Then, leaving the front of the body, shift your awareness to the back of the body... the back of the head... the neck... the shoulders... the upper back... the mid-back... the lower back... the buttocks... the back of the thighs... the calves... the heels of the feet... holding the whole of the back of the body in awareness... staying with this for a few moments.

Now, shifting your attention, become aware of the whole body lying here... the whole body... the sum of all its parts... however they may be... the entire body resting in awareness...

A short practice that is best done lying down

MOVING ATTENTION AROUND THE BODY

Our attention can be seen as a flashlight that we can turn one way to get a tightly focused, narrow beam of light or turn the other way to obtain a wider, more diffused beam. **In mindfulness meditation we switch between a narrow focus of attention, such as on a particular part of the body, or a single focus, such as sound, to opening our awareness wider to encompass the whole body or to receive whatever comes into our sphere of attention.** It is important to cultivate both types of attention.

Try this

You can practice narrowing and expanding your beam of awareness with this body-focused exercise, which is best done at home or somewhere you can be private and undisturbed. If you are just focusing on your hand, for example, you can do it sitting down. But if you are going to practice with your whole body, I would suggest lying down so you feel comfortable, warm, and supported.

You can make the exercise as long or as short as you like. For example, a short practice could be as follows:

Beginning by placing your awareness in a single toe, hold it in your mind's eye… resting your attention in this location… noticing any sensations that may be present (or the absence of sensation). The act of tuning in is important.

Then, expand to include all the toes on one foot… being curious about each individual toe and how it is in this moment… then the sole of the foot… the heel… the weight of the heel and the foot touching the surface.

Each time, focus the attention on that specific part of the body and if your mind gets pulled away by thoughts (which it most likely will), just bringing it back to your place of attention…

And then widen it out and experience a sense of the whole foot… holding the foot in your mind's eye and just being aware of it, noticing whether there are any physical sensations or not... noticing any sense of temperature... any internal sensations... any external sensations, such as a breeze or fabric touching skin. If you would like to, you can also direct the breath into the foot, breathing in and breathing out of the foot—as if the foot was breathing.

You could make it a longer practice by starting with the toes on one foot, working around the different areas and then holding the whole foot in awareness... next, letting go of the foot and beginning to move up the different parts of the leg, followed by holding the whole leg, including the foot, in awareness, perhaps breathing in and out of it.

Then, you could extend to the other leg, the torso (front and back), the arms, the neck and head and then the whole body.

STANDING TALL
LIKE A MOUNTAIN

Standing Mountain is a traditional yoga pose that is a quick way of mentally "coming to sit"—coming to a state of alert relaxed attention. The pose is **grounded in the earth through the feet, but has a sense of uplift in the upper part of the body and the head.**

This is a practice I often do while I am waiting for a bus or a train, or standing in line, as it is **a good way of practicing coming into the body at any time.** It is also a useful grounding exercise if you are feeling worried or nervous, for example before attending an interview, or waiting for a medical or dental appointment.

Standing Mountain can also be used as "punctuation" or a pause in movement practices, such as walking or yoga. It can be done at any time and anywhere you can stand, and **no one need be aware you are doing it**.

If you are standing firm and solid, you will feel more physically stable—noticing the sensations of contact with the floor/ground will take you out of your head and into your body.

TIP *People often make their hip width too big or too small. To find your correct hip width, stand with your feet parallel and together. Now, keeping your heels fixed, move both sets of toes outward until they reach what would be "ten to two" on a clock. Then, bring each heel into line with the toes.*

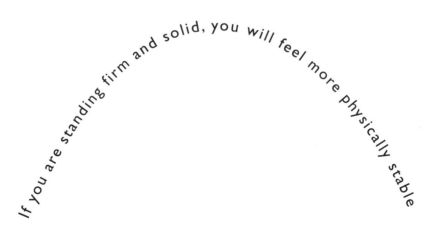

If you are standing firm and solid, you will feel more physically stable

Try this

Stand softly with your feet parallel and hip-width apart, without locking your knees. It can be helpful to take a deep breath in and then, as you breathe out, let the knees soften slightly.

Your arms relaxed at your sides, imagine a silken thread running from the base of the spine, up through the back and the back of the neck and out through the crown of the head… Picture someone pulling gently on this thread so there is a small shift, a sense of the crown of the head lifting to the sky and the chin relaxing down.

You can extend the practice by scanning through the body, perhaps starting with the feet, noticing the soles of the feet in contact with the earth… noticing the toes… Are they relaxed or gripping? Just monitor how they are without any sense of wanting or needing the body to be in a particular state… scanning through the feet, the ankles… the shins and calves… noticing the knees… the thighs and up into the torso…

Now become aware of the pelvis, the belly, the lower back… moving up the spine to notice the shoulders… coming round to the chest… and moving up the neck into the face, the scalp, the whole head…

Stand tall… grounded, connected, taking a stance of alert attention…

See also SITTING MOUNTAIN, PAGES 161–2

STANDING MOVEMENT PRACTICE

Standing Mountain (see pages 57–9) is the core element of this standing movement practice. We begin in Standing Mountain, we end with it, and we also return to it at the end of each movement. By interspersing periods of Standing Mountain with movement, we can **notice the effect that movement has on the body, as well as the differences and similarities of movement versus stillness**.

Movement practices are an opportunity to **become more familiar with the body**—particularly the body in this moment. This will be different from how it was yesterday and how it may be tomorrow. Honoring those differences is important. In mindful movement practices we are paying attention to physical sensations and **being curious about what happens to the body when we move**. We may notice thoughts and emotions arising and these can be labeled for what they are before coming back to the body. We may do this dance back and forward for the entire time and that is the practice. The most important thing when doing mindful movement is to **listen to your body and honor its limitations**. Experiment with the "edge" of resistance but on no account push through it.

Try this

You can do the following practices as individual poses or strung together in a sequence, depending on how much time you have available.

FINDING YOUR CENTER

Start in Standing Mountain (see pages 57–9), with your arms at your sides, keeping the knees soft, and take your attention down into your feet. Become aware of your feet connecting with the earth... grounded... supported...

Maintaining that solid connection with the ground, begin to lean forward slightly from the ankles... coming back to center... then repeating... each time exploring the point where the lean could become a fall forward (I call this "the edge" of forward.) If you need to, you can take a step forward to maintain your balance.

Now, if it feels okay, begin to explore "the edge" of backward. Remembering that these are really small movements, gently sway forward, keeping your lower legs and feet firmly grounded... then sway backward... in between, coming to center...

Then, begin to do the same thing but this time exploring "the edge of sideways"...

Always come back to center... perhaps standing still for a second or two when you reach this position and exploring what being centered feels like. Experiment with the degree of movement… starting small… becoming larger… and then coming back smaller and smaller until you are standing still.

Throughout the practice notice what is happening with the breath… noticing the muscles in the body tensing and relaxing.

You can go through a similar process—using the upper body alone—when you first come to sit, by rocking from side to side for a few seconds before settling at your center.

STRETCH AND SIDEWAYS BEND

Start in Standing Mountain, then, shifting your weight to the left side of the body, on your next in-breath, let the right arm float upward. Let it go as far as it likes, following the length of the in-breath, and when this turns into an out-breath, relax the body, but keep the right arm raised while feeling the shoulder drop down.

On your next in-breath… reaching the right arm up to the sky, feel the stretch down the whole length of the body, and then on the out-breath bend the right arm over the head… keeping the body upright as if you are standing between two parallel sheets of glass. Stay in this position for a breath or two, noticing what happens when you breathe out and what happens in the body when you breathe in… noticing any thoughts or emotions arising… but continually bringing the attention back to the body.

Now, on the next in-breath lift the right arm back up so it is shooting toward the sky. Breathing out as you relax the shoulder, then breathing in again… and then as you are breathing out, letting the arm float back down to the side. Stay in Standing Mountain for a breath or two, noticing what is happening in the body, before doing the whole sequence on the opposite side of the body.

BALANCING POSE

From Standing Mountain, shift your weight over to one side, lifting the opposite foot 1–2in (2.5–5cm) off the floor. If it is helpful, you can balance the lifted foot against the standing leg. It is fine to do this pose standing against a wall for extra balance. It is also helpful to find a static spot directly in front of you and gaze at it. Experiment with the position of your arms—you can hold them stretched out at each side, or place them on your hips, or bring them in front of you palm to palm.

As you balance on one leg, notice how much movement is involved in standing still… how balancing involves a constant readjustment of position—we often need to start over as we put a foot down and take the position again.

Come back into Standing Mountain with both feet planted firmly on the ground. Then change legs and do the pose on the other side. End in Standing Mountain.

TWIST

Starting in Standing Mountain, with your feet parallel, knees soft, and your hips facing forward, begin turning at the waist to one side. Make sure you keep your hips and knees facing forward, even if this means you don't twist so far. You can fold your arms one on top of the other and lead the movement with the elbow, keeping your gaze fixed on the tip of the elbow. Then, come back to center... repeat in the opposite direction... again making sure the hips and knees stay facing forward.

You can make this a dynamic movement by coordinating it with the breath—experiment with doing a movement on an in-breath or an out-breath, and noticing the difference.

Do this slowly a few times but then, if you'd like to, let go of the arms so they are hanging at your sides, and begin moving from side to side, gradually speeding up... keeping the knees soft and facing forward... but letting the arms gently bang against the lower back as you softly twist at the waist to one side, then the other.

TO FINISH

At the end of a movement practice, remain in Standing Mountain posture for a moment and perhaps scan through the body again as you did at the start, before focusing on the breath for a minute or two.

SITTING DOWN
MOVEMENT PRACTICE

This is a short movement practice that you can do at your desk or sitting on a firm kitchen or dining chair. You can do the whole thing or any section on its own.

In all mindful movement practices **we are noticing physical sensations and are curious about what happens when we move**. We may notice thoughts and emotions arising and these can be labeled for what they are before bringing our attention back to the body. We may do this dance back and forward all through the practice—that is the practice. **The most important thing when doing mindful movement is to listen to your body and to respect its limitations**. Experiment with the "edge" of resistance if you wish, but on no account push through it. There is no competition with ourselves or others.

> *Movement practice is an opportunity to become more familiar with the body—particularly in this moment. This will be different from how the body was yesterday and how it may be tomorrow. Honoring these differences is important.*

Try this

Begin with your feet planted on the floor, then bending forward so you are touching your toes, push the buttocks to the back of the chair seat and come back up to sit. You should now be sitting tall and upright.

Experiment with your eyes open and/or closed.

THE HEAD AND THE NECK

Looking straight ahead (imagining that there is a silken thread running up the back of the spine, neck and head, which is being pulled gently so the crown of the head rises and the chin is tucked in)... breathe in and then as you begin to breathe out, turn your head very slowly to the right... coming back to the center on the in-breath... and then as you are breathing out, turning the head to the left... breathing in coming back to center. Repeat this three times.

Taking your attention to your right ear, hold it in awareness, just letting it float down toward the shoulder. There is no expectation that the ear will reach the shoulder. Feel the stretch down the opposite side of the neck, then come back to center and repeat on the left hand side.

(There's no need for the shoulder to get involved, so if you feel it tensing or moving upward, just pause, breathing in and out a few times and letting the shoulder float back down.)

Looking straight ahead (remembering the silken thread…), just imagine that the crown of the head is really heavy, letting it nod slowly forward… lead with the head, your eyes are closed… just let it nod forward toward the chest while you are breathing in and breathing out… noticing the sense of contraction as well as expansion. When you feel as if you have gone as far as you would like to, just pause there, breathing in and breathing out for a few rounds before coming back up as slowly as you went down.

With your head relaxed and centered, imagine you have a blob of paint on the end of your nose and that there is a pane of glass or wall directly in front of you. Begin by painting very small circles with your nose… experimenting with going slowly and then faster, as well as with the size of the circle, but always being mindful of what feels comfortable and not making any sudden jerky movements. Reverse the direction.

THE SHOULDERS AND THE CHEST

Sitting up tall in the chair, rising out of the waist, clasp your hands behind your back and push away from the body… stretch… feeling the shoulder blades coming closer together and the chest opening. Relax and repeat.

Bringing your fingertips to your shoulders and then taking your attention to your elbows, slowly move the elbows to the front, bringing them together and then apart… in the same position, with the fingers on the shoulders… moving the elbows in a small, gentle, circular pattern, first one way and then the other.

Sitting up tall, with your hands clasped behind your head, keeping the hips, knees and feet square and facing forward, twist from the waist first one way and then come back and go the other way. Perhaps pause at the point where you feel you have gone as far as you can and just breathe… in and out… noticing the experience. Repeat the sequence three times.

Again ensuring you are sitting up tall, bring your elbows close to your rib cage with your lower arms and hands out directly in front of you, palms upward. Keeping the elbows tucked in, breathe out as you move the hands outward… only going as far as you can without moving the elbows (and this may not be very far)… feeling the stretch and the opening of the chest, then coming back on an in-breath and repeating. Repeat three times.

Sitting up tall, this time with your hands on your hips, bringing the elbows together behind you (but without any expectation that they will ever meet), feel the shoulder blades moving together, feel the chest opening up… Repeat three times.

THE HANDS

Many of us spend a disproportionate amount of time, whether it is for work or leisure, at a keyboard. It is only fair to give your hands and fingers a regular workout to counteract the negative effects of this.

Lifting your right hand, allow your wrist to go limp. Let the wrist and hand go loose and floppy... perhaps gently shaking the wrist so it hangs down vertically, its weight heavy.

Begin moving one finger at a time, as if the fingers are doing a mini Mexican wave... folding them into the palm and then extending them out again. Do this both slowly and fast... experimenting with the difference (leaving the thumb out of the picture for now.)

Then, stretch the thumb to its full length and fold it in... repeat a few times.

Now, taking the attention back to the wrist, begin rotating the wrist in one direction and then in the other... getting as full an extension as you can, but always being wise to the limitations of your body. There is no specific goal. Repeat the sequence on the opposite hand.

FINALLY, SIT AND BREATHE WITH AWARENESS OF THE WHOLE BODY.

CULTIVATING BODY AWARENESS

Deliberately turning our attention to our physical experience is a way of cultivating increased body awareness, practicing being with physical sensations, and **cultivating an attitude of curiosity and interest in our physical experience**. If we practice this regularly, we will find it easier to **turn to the body when we are experiencing emotional upset or stuck in a thinking rut**.

The action of noticing what is going on in the body occupies the same neural "highway" as ruminative thought, so **turning our attention to the body is a way of deliberately shifting gears, taking us away from the mind and our thoughts**.

If we do this regularly, we will also become familiar with our body—what is "normal" for us—and so will find it easier to notice any changes and imbalances sooner rather than later.

Cultivate an attitude of curiosity

Try this

Finding a space that is quiet and where you will not be disturbed, sit in the way that feels most comfortable for you (see pages 39–40.)

Take a few moments to settle into your seat. Adjust your position and make sure the lower part of the body is firmly grounded and connected to the floor or chair and, at the same time, rise up out of the waist with the crown of the head lifting toward the ceiling and your chin tucked in. You should feel alert yet relaxed.

Begin by taking your attention to the breath. Focus your attention on the part of the body where you feel the breath most strongly and rest your attention there… staying with the length of each in-breath… noticing the pause as the in-breath becomes an out-breath… and then staying with the out-breath. Continue in this way for a few minutes, simply experiencing the sensations of breathing, whatever they may be in this moment. If judgments arise, acknowledge their presence and firmly escort the attention back to the breath.

Notice if the breath is deep or shallow, rapid or slow, but letting go of any need to be breathing in a particular way. Just let yourself breathe without trying to change it (although it may change, and that's okay)… simply being curious about your breath in this moment.

After a while, expand your awareness to include the whole body. Become aware of the points of contact with the floor (the soles of the feet or your buttocks)…

noticing sensations of weight, contact, hardness, softness, texture… Perhaps scan upward through the body from the feet to the crown of the head. What do you notice?

Now, settle into an awareness of the body. You may be strongly aware of the breath or perhaps of physical sensations that arise, with the breath in the background.

The attitudes we are trying to cultivate are ones of curiosity, interest, and friendliness. Explore the body as if it is a new friend that you want to get to know a little better. What are you discovering today?

If a particular sensation starts calling for your attention, you have choice of what to do:

* You can deliberately focus in on the sensation and explore it… What is it like? Where exactly is it? Is it changing or constant? How would you describe it—throbbing, itching, pounding, stabbing…? If it were a color, what would it be? What happens when you pay attention to this sensation? Gather information about the experience rather than analyzing it.

∗ You can turn your attention to the breath, using it as an anchor for your attention. Every time you are pulled away by the physical sensations, simply come back to the breath (and you can do this over and over again.)

∗ You can direct the breath into the area of discomfort, imagining that you are breathing in and out from this place.

∗ You can make a decision to adjust your position, but do so mindfully, rather than automatically reacting to the physical sensation. When you need to move, make a deliberate decision to do so and pay attention to the process of moving and settling into a new position.

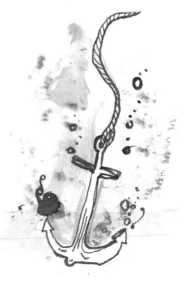

REMEMBER

We never want to sit through pain. **We can practice being with discomfort**, but we do so with kindness and compassion. So we might **stay with an uncomfortable sensation** for only a second or two, but gradually we may find we can allow it to be there longer without reacting to it.

We always work at a pace that feels right for us—and **what we do today may be different from what we did yesterday** or what we will do tomorrow. Practice "beginner's mind," noticing what is there rather than what we think should be there or what we want to be there.

When you notice the urge to move and end the practice, try exploring this further—can you feel it as a sensation in the body? Play with **experiencing the impulse without acting on its demands**. What does this feel like?

And when you want to finish, make a deliberate decision to do so and **end with a moment or two of focusing on the breath** before expanding the awareness back out to include the body and your immediate environment.

WALKING WITH NOWHERE TO GO

Usually when we walk it is with a sense of purpose — we may be exercising the dog, going to work, or accompanying the children to school. Whatever the reason **we rarely walk just for the sake of walking**.

Walking practice is a way of moving out of the mind and into the body and it is a good choice if you are feeling restless or anxious, and sitting feels like too much of a challenge. Also if you are feeling sleepy, you are more likely to remain awake walking rather than sitting.

So often when we are walking in everyday life we are going from A to B on autopilot. Therefore in walking practice we tend to **walk slowly in order to remind ourselves that we are doing something different**. It is not that walking practice is holy or sacred, it is simply that it is easier to be present when we change the way we normally walk.

You can do this practice at home or even outside if there is somewhere private where you will be unobserved. We often do this practice in a circle, as this emphasizes that **we are walking without any destination in mind**, but your "circle" could just as easily consist of an elongated oval if you don't have a large amount of space. **Doing this practice barefoot can help strengthen the sense of connection between the foot and the floor or ground.**

Try this

Begin in Standing Mountain pose (see pages 57–9), with the feet parallel and hip-width apart. Your arms can be relaxed by your sides, or folded or clasped in front or behind you. Your eyes should be open.

Feel your feet connecting with the floor, the weight of the body being held and supported… connecting with the breath… becoming aware of standing…

Next, taking your attention down into either foot (it does not matter which), shift your weight on to the opposite leg as you begin to slowly peel the heel off the floor. Feel the transition of weight… lifting the foot… shifting it… and placing it down… noticing the movement, the sense of weight, the experience of the foot touching the floor…

Become aware of the different parts of the body involved in the process of putting one foot in front of the other…

Then, switch the attention to the other foot and go through the process again… lifting… shifting… placing—you can repeat these words silently to yourself if you find it helpful.

Every time your mind goes for a walk, just bring it back and place your attention back on the feet. You will probably have to do that over and over again, and that is okay.

When you come to a stop, assume Standing Mountain for a moment or two, and perhaps scan through the body and notice how it is now.

walk slowly in order to remind ourselves that we are doing something different

chapter 3

CULTIVATING WELL-BEING

We all want to be happy, but we often mistake a rush of excitement for happiness. **Well-being is more of a sense of contentment, peacefulness, and connection with a place and people.** We can feel a sense of connection with the world and people around us even when we are suffering from illness and experiencing difficulties.

The practices in this section **focus on paying attention to ordinary activities in our daily lives**—such as showering and washing dishes. These are the kind of activities that we do repeatedly and, as such, they slide into obscurity, each merging into the next, losing its unique identity. Oftentimes we are on automatic pilot to the degree that we look back and have no recollection of the process of getting up and going out of the door. In this way we lose the moments that make up our life and once lost, they are gone forever. **By paying attention to these regular activities, we can reclaim the lost minutes of our day**, and we can connect more deeply with our life.

We can also reconnect with the world around us—by noticing the sky, the earth below our feet, and the people around us. Looking beyond ourselves, **we can gain a wider perspective on our own life and our place on this planet.**

MINDFUL EATING

When I was small, I used to eat really slowly. However, **going to boarding school** changed all that; there, if you wanted second helpings, you had to be quick off the mark and **mealtimes were a time for socializing** rather than for savoring the food you were eating. The consequence was that **I soon got into the habit of eating quickly without paying much attention to the food.**

The stomach takes about 20 minutes to let the brain know that we are full, so if we eat too quickly, that message arrives after we have already eaten too much.

Mindful eating reminds us how ordinary meditation can be

In addition, **if we eat fast, we don't savor the food properly because it is not in our mouth long enough** for us to be fully aware of the textures and the changes in taste. This also applies when we combine eating with other activities, such as talking or watching television.

Bringing mindfulness to eating also reminds us how ordinary meditation can be—it really is within the reach of every one of us.

Try this

Mindful eating is best done in silence, although you can do it with others if they remain silent, too. Maintaining silence in this practice reminds us that we are doing something differently—in this case, that we are eating a meal in a way we usually don't.

Silence is often like an "on" switch. Without the interruptions of talking and listening, we naturally pay attention to what we are eating, and as we pay attention we slow down accordingly. We notice how the body reacts in anticipation of the next spoonful. We chew our food rather than swallow it automatically. Perhaps we feel the stomach expanding and becoming fuller with every mouthful. We pause between mouthfuls. We are aware of the crunchy texture of this carrot; the juiciness of that tomato; the delicate flavor of this spice, the strong taste of that herb. We become aware of what we are eating.

BRING CURIOSITY AND EXPLORATION TO THE ACT OF EATING:

* What do you see?

* What can you smell?

* What does it feel like?

* What can you hear?

* What can you taste?

As we **become aware of what we are putting into our mouths** we begin to make deliberate choices. If we are **focusing on tasting our food,** we want it to taste as good as it can be. We **begin noticing how we feel after certain foods** and naturally gravitate toward those that give us energy rather than make us feel sluggish. Also, **we become aware of the point of choice** when we are reaching for something—this gives us time to pause and **make a conscious decision about what we are going to eat,** rather than eating mindlessly.

Focus on tasting our food...

become aware of the point of choice...

DRINKING TEA

Often when we **take time out to sit down and have a cup of tea or coffee** it is not the peaceful interlude we had anticipated but rather an opportunity to think about our "To Do" list or to replay some slight or hurt that we have received or doled out.

Vietnamese meditation teacher Thich Nhat Hahn suggests **drinking tea to drink tea** (and of course it can be applied to any drink.)

Try This

Sitting down, be with your cup of tea. Explore the tea with your senses...
feeling the heat of the cup against your hands...
drinking in the scent of the leaves (perhaps experiment with herbal teas)
... noticing the color of the liquid... perhaps the odd leaf floating around...

becoming aware of the movement of bringing the cup to your lips, noticing any
physical response in anticipation... experiencing the taste... noticing whether
there is an ahh of pleasure or a shudder of distaste (and remembering that
we are not trying to have a particular experience, instead we are just
being with this experience)...

Whenever your mind gets pulled away by thoughts (which it will), just noticing
where you have gone and then coming back, kindly and gently to the body
and the sensations you felt.

REALLY DRINK YOUR TEA.

WHO ARE YOU
SHOWERING WITH?

Most of us **spend much of our time thinking of the past or the future**, thereby paying no attention to the present. Constantly going over your "To Do" list, or worrying about how you could have done things differently, **keeps the body in a state of vigilance and, sometimes, anxiety**.

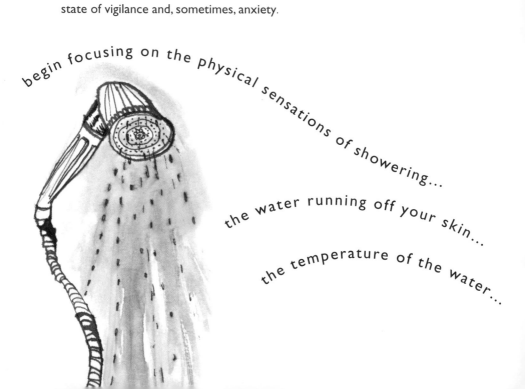

begin focusing on the physical sensations of showering...

the water running off your skin...

the temperature of the water...

Try this

When you shower in the morning, take a moment or two to notice who has "joined" you... Who are you thinking about—perhaps it is your boss, or colleagues at work, maybe it is someone you are going to see later that day, or perhaps it is someone you talked to yesterday. It might be your partner, your children, your parents, your next-door neighbor... How many people are in the shower with you?

Then, begin focusing on the physical sensations of showering... the water running off your skin... the temperature of the water... the soap lathering up between your fingers. Notice when you experience a sensation of delight or when there might be a feeling of pushing away or dislike. There is no right way to shower and whether we are invigorating ourselves first thing in the morning, simply shampooing our hair, or cooling off after a hot day, all we are doing is paying attention to the act of taking a shower.

TIP Identifying who turns up in the shower regularly may give you some helpful feedback on where your preoccupations are at any one time.

DOING THE DISHES
TO DO THE DISHES

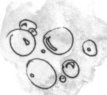

Meditation teacher Thich Nhat Hahn describes "washing the dishes in order to wash the dishes"—that is, **doing an activity that might be considered boring and giving it your full attention.** Thich Nhat Hahn says that too often we rush through the action of washing the dishes solely to get to the end result (clean dishes) and perhaps to then reward ourselves with a relaxing cup of tea. Yet when we sit down to drink the tea, we do so without any sense of enjoyment as **we have already moved on our attention to the next thing.**

When we focus on what we are doing, we often discover an interest in it. I have found, too, that how I approach the activity informs my relationship with it. If I am forced or feel obliged to do something, I feel resentful and resistant to it. But if I **make a conscious choice to do an activity**—even if it is not something I want to do—I am approaching it from a different perspective and **what happens next is affected by this change.**

> *You can bring a similar, deliberate awareness to those activities that you do regularly without paying attention—for example, cleaning your teeth, getting dressed, shaving, and so on. When you have done these activities so many times, you lose interest in them and tend to "zone out." To break this habit, do them differently. Perhaps slow down or change your routine—for example, if you usually start brushing your teeth at the front, try beginning at the back (your dentist will appreciate this!) Use your senses to explore the activity. You don't have to spend much longer than you usually would, but by doing the activity differently, you can reclaim lost minutes of your day and lost hours of your life.*

Try this

Choose a household activity that you normally find dull. It could be washing the dishes or taking out the garbage… or anything similar.

Take a moment to pay attention to what you are feeling… any sensations in the body? Any stiffness, tension, or tightness? What thoughts are present? Are there any emotions arising? Notice whatever is present and acknowledge it, mentally saying, "I see you."

Next, make a deliberate decision to do the chosen activity, even if you don't want to, and acknowledge the choice you are making despite not having any expectation of enjoying it.

Then, carry out the activity… always paying attention to sensations felt in the body. Notice any emotions and any stories you might be telling yourself.

Whenever you notice a sense of wanting to be somewhere else or doing something different, just bring yourself back to this moment, this activity now. You don't have to enjoy the activity, just be present in it.

Afterward reflect on your experience.

SPORTS AND LEISURE ACTIVITIES

Many sportsmen and women are using **mindfulness** as they find it **helps with concentration and focus**. I have introduced mindfulness into many areas of my life and **the rewards have often been unexpected**. Here is an example that illustrates the benefits, as well as providing guidelines for introducing mindfulness into a sport, but the principles can be applied to any leisure activity.

RUNNING

I took up running after reading Danny Dreyer's *Chi Running* and I realized I could **use mindfulness to turn running into a meditation practice**. In *Chi Running*, the focus is on the body and its posture, noticing body alignment and making adjustments to prevent injury (which, incidentally, also increases speed.) **The emphasis is on a gradual process** and on starting from where you are now (even if this is not where you would like to be.) Although I am a relative beginner—and a slow one at that—I now love running. I love the sense of community I receive from running in London's Hyde Park and seeing the same faces from time to time; the city is no longer anonymous. **I feel connected to the city**: passing the King's Troop on the way to the Changing of the Guard, tourists scratching their heads as they puzzle over a map, the marathon runners pounding out their training hours. I love feeling the weather on my face and experiencing the seasons changing. I enjoy seeing what my body is capable of and, although I am slow, I work the "edge" of what I can do, and **recognize that every "running" day is different from the one before**. I have learned the importance of listening to my body to avoid the risk of injuring myself.

Try this

Paying attention to your experience means paying attention to what is arising in terms of sensations felt, thoughts, and emotions. How are you doing your chosen activity? Are you giving yourself a hard time because you are not running fast enough or haven't produced a masterpiece or because you have dropped a stitch? What emotions are arising as you do this activity? What sensations are you feeling in the body? Be curious about your experience.

When we do any activity mindfully we let go of any attachment to a particular outcome and instead focus on the process. Paradoxically, letting ourselves off the hook in terms of achieving a particular goal often means we are more relaxed and thus able to have a different experience with more favorable results. But more significant, perhaps, is that we will almost certainly have had a richer and more fulfilling experience and be more aware of what is going on in our body, which is helpful both in terms of technique and injury prevention

> Why not experiment? Perhaps do your chosen activity as usual one day and another day do it with mindfulness. Reflect on and record your experiences on both occasions. What can you learn from your observations?

PREPARING A MEAL

Paying attention to food while we are preparing it is **a way of turning a chore into a sensory experience**. The following practice is **best done with fresh foods that feed the senses**—particularly, sight and smell—such as salad ingredients.

Try this

You can begin this practice when you are out shopping, choosing items for your salad. Notice the colors of the vegetables and fruit piled up next to each other. Separate the different smells... for example, notice the sharp tang of fresh herbs. Feel the different textures. Notice any sense of moving toward "Mmmm, I like these..." versus a sense of resistance or pushing away of foods you like less "Yuk... I don't like these," and doing this in the context of noticing what these different states feel like physically rather than judging that either one is good or bad.

When you are ready to prepare your food, focus all your attention on what you are doing. Turn off the television or the radio, avoid talking with others, and give your undivided attention to preparing the food.

As you chop, cut, slice, and dice, open up the senses to the experience. Whenever your mind wanders, simply notice where it has gone and escort it back.

Prepare your meal with a spirit of creating a feast of art... mixing colors, textures, tastes, and smells together.

THEN, SIT DOWN,
EAT, AND ENJOY.

GIVING THANKS

Becoming aware of all that is good in our lives is a way of cultivating positive feelings of well-being. We can **extend thanks toward those people who have influenced us in a positive way.** This might include parents, teachers, and friends, as well as doctors, nurses, the person who helped you find something in the store, and the stranger who gave you directions when you were lost. This practice is **a way of connecting with those people**—known and unknown—who have done you a service in some way and who deserve your thanks.

Try this

You can do this practice somewhere private, or on a train or a bus. Sit comfortably and bring to mind someone in your life to whom you feel gratitude. Perhaps they have done something specific for you, or have supported you, or made a difference in your life. Picture this person and, opening your heart, send them wishes of kindness and thanks, as you acknowledge your gratitude for their presence in your life. You may make up your own phrases or use ones such as:

"Thank you" or "Thank you for… (you fill in the blank)" or "Thank you for being a part of my life."

Then bring to mind another person and do the same thing. Extend the practice to as many people as you like, according to the amount of time you have.

Keep a Gratitude Journal and each night jot down a short list of anything or anyone you felt grateful for that day. Keep it simple and specific. This can be a powerful practice that connects us to the many small things in life for which we can be grateful for.

SPACIOUS SKY

As a child I would lie flat on my back on the grass and **watch the sky, and the clouds moving overhead**. I felt the contact with the earth—a warmth—as well as the scratchiness of the grass touching my bare skin. I remember **experiencing a connection with the earth, but at the same time feeling a sense of the spaciousness of the sky and of the universe beyond.**

Try this

Either sit, stand, or lie down somewhere outside where you have a good view of the sky. (It does not matter if at the edges buildings or trees creep in.) Taking a few minutes to ground yourself, feel a sense of connection with the earth through the feet, buttocks, and any other points of contact. Notice the sensations of being supported.

Turning your eyes to the sky above, open your vision to receive whatever passes across it... clouds... airplanes... vapor trails... birds... Notice if the mind is pulled away and, if so, at that moment of awareness, bring it back to the sense of connection with the ground and the spaciousness of the sky above. Open yourself up to the sky... this sky that continues unbroken across land and sea, countries and continents... this sky that has no boundaries, that is never-ending. But also try to maintain a sense of connection with the earth throughout.

OPENING UP TO
THE UNIVERSE

In our light-polluted world there are few chances to **appreciate the vastness of a truly dark night sky**. The boundaries of our world can feel small and contracted. When neighborhood lights blaze, highlighting differences and marking borders, the boundaries of our world are emphasized.

Try this

To connect with a wider world seize any opportunity you can to sit, or better still, to lie on the ground and look directly up into the night sky.

Feel the earth beneath you... holding and supporting you... breathing in... breathing out... allowing yourself to be held and supported... grounded in this earth... safe in this moment... yet spinning in the vastness.

Breathing in... breathing out... Expand your awareness to include whatever comes into your line of sight... the lights of a plane... a blinking satellite... letting go of any stories or thoughts that might be arising about them.

Breathing in... breathing out... Expand your awareness further to include the stars ... the planets... the galaxies... breathing in... breathing out... Soak in the dark night of space... bathe in the starlight.

Breathing in... breathing out... Feel the earth beneath you... breathing with the earth... breathing in... breathing out... connecting with the ground... connecting through time... connecting across the galaxy... connecting with the universe... at one with this earth.

"SEEING-DRAWING"

In my experience **there are many links between drawing and meditation.** To draw accurately you have to see what is actually there—not what you think is there—you pay attention to the subject and really look. And **the more you look, the more you see**. If you can let the critical mind fall away, you can enter a mode of being where **the drawing draws itself** and there is no sense of "I," just **lines or shapes**

that interrelate. We quickly realize that **everything**, however dull it might seem at first glance, **is worthy of our interest**, and through "seeing-drawing" everything has a beauty all of its own.

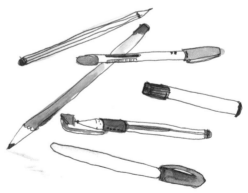

Try this

You don't need to have any drawing experience to try this exercise in Blind Contour Drawing developed by Kimon Nicolaides. Pick up a pencil and a piece of paper and find something to draw—a crumpled up tissue, a feather, a complex flower (the more complicated the better.)

Position yourself so the paper is on the table and your drawing hand is over it, but your head is turned away and you are looking at your object, whatever that may be.

Begin by looking at the object before settling your gaze on one of its edges, and very, very slowly, move your eye along that edge and at the same time move the pencil. Don't lift your pencil off the paper. Don't worry about what the pencil is actually doing and do not turn and look at the drawing.

Continue doing this for as long as you can—a minimum of five minutes if possible (you can set a timer if you like)—but ideally longer. Don't turn your head and look, just keep the eye and the hand moving slowly, as if you were an ant crawling along the surface, feeling the ups and downs, the twists and turns of the edge.

You cannot do this exercise too slowly. Wherever your eye follows an edge, your pencil will follow. When you have finished, your "drawing" will look nothing like the object, but you will have experienced seeing the object in a totally new way.

Try this

This second "seeing-drawing" practice is similar to the first, but this time we are going to shift our attention back and forward between the paper and the object.

Begin with a simple object, such as a leaf. Settle into your drawing position, pick up your object in your hand, and just gaze at it. Look and pay attention to the object. After a few minutes, place it on your paper, close your eyes, and visualize it. Holding your pencil in your hand ready to make a mark, picture the object in your mind's eye.

Open your eyes and look once more at your object. Look and see, and begin moving your pencil as you move your eyes. Your pencil is an extension of your senses—it moves as if you are touching the object, following its contours, dipping into its hollows, twisting and turning across and around.

You are only drawing what your eye sees. Let go of any judging of what you are drawing. When your attention wanders, stop. Only move the pencil when your eye is moving over the object.

BEING WITH THE GOOD

Our evolutionary survival mechanism is primed to remember bad experiences so they serve as warnings for the future, whereas pleasant experiences serve no such purpose and thus are discarded. **Many of us also indulge in black-and-white thinking. We catastrophize**: "I've had a terrible day," we say, tarring the whole day with negativity, when **the reality is that each day is made up of a multitude of experiences** positive, negative, and neutral. If we can start to **pay attention and notice**, particularly when we have **a positive experience**, and hold that experience in our being for two or three seconds, our memory will then "bank" it rather than let it slide away into oblivion. An additional benefit is that noticing a positive experience as it happens makes our life feel richer.

Try this

Make an intention to notice any pleasant experiences you have today. These are going to be mainly small things, such as noticing the clean, sharp smell of air when you leave a stuffy room; hearing a child laugh or a favorite song; seeing a pleasing arrangement of colors, and so on. It will be different for each one of us.

When you become aware of a pleasant experience, first notice what it feels like in the body. Does it feel tight, contracted, loose or open? If you were asked to describe it, what words or pictures would you use? What thoughts do you notice? What emotions are present?

Remember, we are not trying to create positive experiences. We are simply paying attention to any pleasant experiences that regularly occur but that we usually ignore or quickly forget.

ALL THAT IS RIGHT WITH ME

Culturally, we tend to focus on what is wrong with us—what we can't do, what we want to improve or change, and so on. **What if we did something totally different and deliberately noticed how much is right with us?**

This practice can be as long or as short as you care to make it. You could do it sitting or lying down, or even while walking.

Try this

Take a moment or two to focus on the sensations of breathing, connecting with the ground through your feet or buttocks… coming into your body.

Start with the most obvious things—the things we take for granted—the feet that carry us, our hands, our sight, our hearing, our sense of taste.

It can be helpful to scan through the body… starting with the feet and then moving upward, making it as detailed or as general as you wish.

As you focus your awareness on each part of the body in turn, notice any thoughts or emotions arising around it. Even if the body's ability to function is less than perfect, or the appearance is not as you would like it to be, just notice what you can do with it, however modest that might be.

Always **start with the simplest of things** that you can do, such as essential skills that you use everyday. Through this practice, we are opening up to the possibility that **there is much that is good or even just okay in our lives**, even when things become difficult.

chapter 4

MAKING
CONTACT

Meditating is often perceived as a solitary pursuit. However, **practicing mindfulness meditation can do much to enhance your relationships** with family, friends, and colleagues.

Mindfulness helps us **see more clearly our patterns of behavior and thinking**, and once we have seen them and brought them into our awareness, **we are better placed to change them**. So, taking the time to practice skills that will help us to be less reactive and more responsive, less distracted and more present, can only be beneficial to those with whom we have contact.

The practices in this section are about cultivating better relationships: with people, our surroundings, and most importantly, with ourselves. **If we cannot show kindness and compassion to ourselves, how can we possibly show it to other people?** The Loving Kindness practices on pages 128–39 help redress this balance.

We are all constantly involved in relationships with others, whether with loved ones or with passing strangers in the street, and so **it is worth reflecting that every interaction we have has an effect**, and that these effects ripple outward to touch many people. Through mindfulness practices **we can work to make our interactions have a more positive effect**, both on ourselves and others.

YOU AND YOUR BABY

Practicing mindfulness while you are pregnant can be particularly helpful. At this time **your body is going through all kinds of changes**, both internally and externally, and **you are likely to be thinking about the future**, which can be quite stressful. Practicing mindfulness of breathing in advance of the birth may be helpful, too.

This practice is a good way to connect with your baby and your body.

If you would like to do this practice with a partner, you can sit or lie side by side and each place one hand over your heart and the other over your pregnant belly.

Try this

Lie down or sit in a comfortable and supported position, and take your attention to the breath. Take a few moments to focus on the part of the body where you feel the breath most strongly and just feel the sensations of breathing.

Then, place one hand on your belly to connect with your baby and the other over your heart, and take your attention to the palms of your hands. Feel the sensations of touching bare skin or cloth, becoming aware of temperature... of warmth or coolness... and also of any sensations of movement or vibration...

Remember that you are not setting out to feel anything and there is no expectation of feeling anything specific, such as your own or the baby's heartbeat, but rather this is just a process of connecting with each other.

PARENTING PRACTICE

Parents often struggle more than most to find time for formal practice, but luckily children present endless opportunities for informal practice. Whether we are faced with a crying baby in the middle of the night or a recalcitrant teenager, parents can feel frustrated and angry, as well as a sense of failure. It is in moments like these that practicing mindfulness can be of benefit to both you and your children.

Try this

In moments of difficulty stop and pause. This can be a literal stopping (which might help prevent an automatic response) or a metaphorical one, but the effect is the same.

Pause and come to the body, taking your attention to any sensations you feel, being curious about what is arising and where, but letting go of any need to analyze "why."

Next, notice what emotions are arising—and there are often more than one. For example, anger may be masking fear, so take a few moments repeatedly to ask yourself, "What is here?" and name it.

Then, becoming aware of the stories you are telling yourself—the "bad parent," the "failing child," and so on)… acknowledge exactly what you are feeling right now, even if it feels inappropriate, politically incorrect, or you feel bad that in this moment you really dislike your child.

Be honest about what is arising, acknowledge its presence and breathe with it, allowing the breath to fill the body from the top of your head to the tips of your toes. Let the whole body breathe.

Allow yourself to feel your emotions while you are breathing, and acknowledge your love for your child in spite of present-moment feelings. Allow any conflicting feelings to co-exist, supported by the breath. Acknowledge your vulnerability, your frailty, your best efforts, and again, your love for your child.

RINGING TELEPHONE

The sound of a ringing telephone can conjure up many emotions, depending on what is going on in our lives—particularly if, say, we are waiting to hear the result of medical tests or a job interview.

It is important to realize that **the sound of a phone may unleash a chain reaction of thoughts, emotions, and physical sensations** in us, and what is happening internally will influence how we react to what we hear from the caller.

If we can bring ourselves into the present moment before we answer the phone, becoming aware of its effect and knowing that we are feeling a particular way may help us respond to the call in a measured manner rather than reacting automatically.

At one time or another, we have all experienced the annoying sound of an unanswered telephone—perhaps in the office or while on public transport. You can adapt this practice to use when someone else's telephone is ringing. Notice the sensations you feel in the body, plus any thoughts and emotions arising, and acknowledge and stay with them as best you can. Allow the ringing to simply be a sound.

Try this

When you hear the phone ringing, immediately ask yourself, "What am I feeling right now?" Check the thoughts, emotions, and sensations in the body, naming them (for example, saying to yourself: "Fear is here".) Then, transfer your awareness to the body, either by connecting to the breath or by feeling your feet in contact with the floor. The whole process takes just seconds. Only then, pick up the telephone.

If you know you have a difficult phone call to make, perhaps take a few moments beforehand to do a Breathing Space, see pages 150–1.

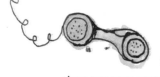

ON HOLD

Being put on hold on the phone can bring up all kinds of thoughts and emotions: **we may be frustrated at the waste of time**, we may perceive it as an insult, we may find the music annoying, and so on.

However, if we can change the way we perceive this, **we can reduce the negative stress it places on the body**. Instead of "waiting" on hold, can we simply "be" on hold?

Why not regard such moments as an opportunity to be with ourselves—a few minutes taken out from work or home life that offer us the chance to **tune in to the body and the breath, and allow us just to be... to be here right now**.

BEING PRESENT IN CONVERSATION

When we communicate with another person, all kinds of information—verbal and nonverbal—is transferred between us. However, **much of the time** we are so determined to get our own point of view across that **we miss what others are saying.** We interrupt and speak over them, or we mentally absent ourselves from listening to them as we rehearse an answer that may no longer be relevant. Moreover, we filter out much of what is said, so **we only hear the words that confirm our particular point of view or story.** We ignore or are unaware of the nonverbal clues that are also offered, because our attention is distracted.

In contrast, when we listen mindfully, we **listen wholeheartedly:** we let the other person speak without interruption and we **really hear what they say before we respond;** we listen with our eyes as well as our ears, noticing nonverbal cues; and we make eye contact. Furthermore, we take time to respond, so we may **pause and notice what effect the words are having on our body** and use that information as invaluable feedback.

Listening mindfully means we often **gain a much clearer and true understanding of what is being said**. We are more aware of our own stories and so acknowledge that there may be bias arising, which we need to take account of. When we listen mindfully, **we feel more connected to the person with whom we are having the conversation**, and they feel more connected to us. We become more aware of our own listening patterns. Becoming aware of our own patterns is the first step toward doing something differently—if that is what is needed (and sometimes it is not.)

Try this

Begin by simply noticing how you usually participate in a conversation. What is your normal mode of listening? (Always remember that you are doing this in a spirit of kindness and learning, rather than one of criticizing or condemning.) Notice, too, how other people listen to you. Do they keep eye contact? Are they multitasking? How does it make you feel if the person you are talking with seems only half-present?

Now, consider how you feel when someone is fully present in a conversation with you. Communicate with others in the same way that you would like them to communicate with you.

* As soon as you realize your mind is wandering, bring it back to listening.

* Avoid interrupting the other person. Let them finish. You will then have heard the complete story rather than only part of it.

* Notice any tendency you have to try to fix things or make them better for the other person, and instead, see if you can just be there for them.

* Avoid multitasking and do just one thing at a time. When you listen, just listen.

* Avoid rehearsing your answers. Listen and then respond. You will find your response will be improved if you have really heard what was said.

* It is okay to pause, take a breath, and pay attention to your body at any time during a conversation.

Remember, we are working to change the habits of a lifetime, so be kind to yourself when you forget or when you butt in to a conversation or interrupt.

SEEING

I love drawing portraits and when you draw someone's face you have to **really look at them and see them**. You are not judging the length of a nose or the size of an ear, but noticing how a certain line aligns with this one, or a particular angle comes down from another, and so on. When you draw  someone you need to **get up close to them and you feel a connection**.

The following practice does not involve any drawing, but it does require looking. Your subject could be another person, a pet, or an inanimate object, such as a flower or a stone, or even a view from a window.

Try this

Take a position where you can see your subject clearly, and settle into your seat. Connect first to the breath and then the body.

Begin looking ahead at the subject. Just open your eyes to whatever comes into your field of vision.

Notice any urge to turn your head in search of something more interesting... but if you do, just bring your head back in the same way that you escort the attention back when the mind wanders. Notice any thoughts arising and let them go or label them as "judging," "planning," "past," or whatever is appropriate.

Rest your eyes on the subject, perhaps letting them roam without turning your head... from time to time, becoming aware of the breath like a radio playing in the background... moving the attention backward and forward in a way that feels right for you. Finish by focusing on the breath.

TOUCHING

This is a companion practice to the Seeing exercise on the previous page. You can do it as a stand-alone practice or before or after Seeing. For this practice you will need an object—it can be anything, natural or man-made, but it is best to use a small object, because you are going to explore it with your hands.

Try this

Choose your object. Sit in front of and within easy reach of it. Assume a comfortable posture (see pages 38–41) and allow the attention to settle on the breath. Connect with the sensations of breathing and the body.

Closing the eyes, take your attention into your hands... becoming aware of the fingers and thumb on one hand... and then of those on the other hand.

Keeping your attention in the body, move the hands to the object and allow them to float down so the tips of the fingers are just in contact with the object's surface. Imagine you have no idea what this object is, whether it is alive or dead, and explore the object by touch. Whenever the mind wanders, bring it back directly to the sense of touch in the fingers and the thumbs.

After a while you may want to pick up the object and explore it in the round, and perhaps involve other senses, such as hearing and smell. Connect with the source of the object—the earth or the people who made it.

When you are ready, place the object back down. Now, take your attention back to the body, and to the hands and fingers and thumbs in particular. Notice what they are like now, after being in contact with the object.

STANDING IN SOMEONE ELSE'S SHOES

Western culture promotes a strong sense of individual identity, but most of us also belong to groups. **Our circle can be as narrow as "me" versus "the rest," though it usually stretches to include family and friends as "us" versus "them,"** and can extend further outward to become our neighborhood/region/country versus another. In general, **"them" represents everyone who is different from us.** Focusing on the differences between us strengthens our own identity and makes it easier to separate ourselves from others. However, the line that separates "us" from "them" is often a fine one, and there is much to be gained from **focusing on what we have in common rather than what makes us different.**

Focus on what we have in common rather than what makes us different

Try this

Sit somewhere quiet where you won't be disturbed and begin by taking a few moments to connect with the breath (see Mindfulness of Breathing, pages 44–5 and 148–149).

Then, bring to mind someone you have come into contact with recently, who you regard as outside your circle, for whatever reason. Notice if your critical mind judges your choice and starts creating a story and, if so, just let it go.

Hold a picture of this person in your mind's eye and begin noticing the characteristics that you share—perhaps you are wearing something the same color as something they are wearing? Or maybe an item of clothing is the same? Working from your head to your toes, identify everything that you have in common with this person—from your gender to your body parts, from your clothing to your hair style.

SIMPLY NOTICE AS MUCH AS YOU CAN, HOWEVER SMALL.
Next, imagine the person as a young child… as someone's son or daughter… perhaps as someone's brother or sister… growing up to be someone's good friend… someone's partner… a mother or a father… a grandmother or a grandfather.

We are not making up things about this person, we are simply acknowledging them as a fellow human being with similar connections, relationships, hopes and fears, joys and sorrows as ourselves. They are simply someone struggling to live a life of happiness, as we all do.

Now, picture yourself standing in this person's shoes… literally feel the shoes they are wearing on your feet. How are these shoes different from the shoes you normally wear? How do your feet feel? Now broaden your awareness to visualize yourself living the life they lead… what does that feel like? What do you notice in terms of sensations arising in your body… emotions… thoughts?

ALTERNATIVE PRACTICE

If you want to do this as an informal practice, when you are out and about, make a point of noticing the people you habitually ignore. These are generally people who serve us in some way—often they wear a uniform. We might label them by their job: waitress, police officer, and so on. We don't usually make eye contact with them and we rarely pause long enough to see the person inside the uniform. So, really look at them. Make eye contact, exchange a greeting. Imagine yourself doing the job they do… how would you like to be treated?

THE EARTH BENEATH US

Recently I was at a public garden. The wet weather had ensured that the lawn was a lush green color, cut to a velvet smooth pile. It begged for bare feet. **The sensations of hot feet touching cool grass**, of sinking into the softness, of the tickle of grass against skin were a pure sensory delight that brought back childhood memories of my grandfather knocking on the window when I dared to run across his pristine lawn. Whether the lawn is lush or parched, **coming directly in contact with the earth is something we don't do often enough as adults.**

Try this

Choose a location that is safe and free from any detritus—it could be a garden or a park—and take off your shoes (and socks if you are wearing them.)

Stand in Mountain pose (see pages 57–9) and take your attention to the soles of the feet. Become aware of your feet in contact with the ground... the sensation of weight, the contact with grass, soil, stones, twigs...

Stand still and know that you are standing.

Then, lift your heels off the ground and let them fall back down, raising first one heel and then the other.

Peel your toes off the ground one by one. Next, feel your feet: the soles, the heels, the toes, the spaces under the arches.

Be aware of your feet touching the earth... this earth that is spinning beneath us, yet feels solid and stable... this earth that connects family, friends, and strangers on one continent with others on another continent...

BRUSHING HAIR

This practice could be done on yourself, a friend or partner, or a child, or perhaps an elderly parent. **It can be a way of connecting emotionally as well as physically with each other** and is also a good practice for getting into the body. If preferred, there is no need for the receiver to know you are doing this as a practice.

While you are doing the brushing, you can focus on the action, feeling the weight of the brush in your hand… noticing how the brushing action changes over time… feeling the sensation of hair touching skin … paying attention to the process of brushing hair.

I would encourage you to let go of any need to count the number of strokes because having a target suggests a goal to reach whereas **in this practice we are exploring the process itself.**

The person whose hair is being brushed can explore the sensations on the scalp… noticing the resonance down through the whole body… softening into the process.

> " In the book Buddha's Brain: The Practical Neuroscience of Happiness, Love and Wisdom, neuropsychologist Rick Hanson describes how monkeys and apes can spend up to six hours a day grooming each other and how research has found that the animal doing the grooming benefited most from the interaction in terms of stress relief. "

CREATING A CIRCLE OF KINDNESS

Offering Loving Kindness to those we care about can be a stand-alone sitting practice or it can form part of a longer practice. It can also be done informally in any quiet space where it is possible to sit and reflect undisturbed.

Try this

Sit and assume a comfortable posture, perhaps taking a few moments to tune in to the breath and allowing yourself to settle.

Bring to mind someone you care about—it may be a partner, a parent, a sibling, a child, or a friend, or even a much-loved pet or animal. Imagine this person or animal and, holding them in your mind's eye, offer them your love and good wishes by silently repeating:

"May you be well,

May you be happy,

May you be free from suffering."

(Remember that it is fine to change the phrases if you wish.)

Repeat each phrase slowly and let it resonate, like a pebble falling down a well...

Now, imagine yourself standing next to the person or the animal, perhaps holding hands with the person or placing your hand on the animal if that feels right to you, and repeating silently:

"May we be well,

May we be happy,

May we be free from suffering."

Then, call to mind someone else you care about, and bring them into your circle and go through the same process.

Continue in this way for as long as you would like to, adding people to your circle and always remembering to include yourself. If you wish, you can end by including all beings.

Notice, too, any thoughts that might arise about the choices you make, monitoring how they resonate in the body, and your emotions. If there is any feeling of contraction or tightening, just notice and acknowledge its presence and remember that you always have a choice of including someone or not.

This is your practice. As you become more experienced and if you wish, you can move on to the Loving Kindness practice that is specifically aimed at people who irritate us (see pages 135–7), but it is always best to **begin with yourself and those you care about.**

"
Many people find it a struggle to offer Loving Kindness to themselves and one way of getting around this is to include yourself when wishing a group of people well, in particular those we care about. "May we be happy" in the context of friends and family often feels appropriate in a way that "May I be happy" does not. By relaxing around the idea of offering Loving Kindness to ourselves within a group, it becomes easier to do Loving Kindness specifically for ourselves (see pages 132–4).
"

OFFERING KINDNESS TO YOURSELF

Many of us are more likely to practice meanness rather than kindness toward ourselves. **We judge ourselves remorselessly, making unreasonable demands on ourselves** and offering no quarter when we fall short. We would never treat someone we cared about in this way. Offering **kindness toward ourselves is an invaluable practice** and one that cannot be done too often. People often worry that they feel nothing when doing practices like this, but that is okay. **There is no expectation to feel anything in particular**, and you should simply continue. Just as a seed grows and puts down roots under the soil long before we see any sign of leaves above ground, so change is happening inside us before we notice any obvious sign of it. If you do this **practice regularly, you will notice a difference**. This practice is commonly done as a sitting practice.

Try this

Sit in a posture in which you feel alert yet relaxed, grounded, and stable. Begin by taking a few moments to connect with the breath. Place your attention wherever in the body you feel the breath most strongly, and just notice the physical sensations of breathing. Remember that the breath is your home base—the place to come back to if at any time things get difficult or you lose your way.

If you would like to, place one hand over the heart. Take a few moments to feel the connection of palm to chest—noticing the sensations of contact, temperature, and movement.

Now, begin repeating two or three phrases such as:

"May I be happy,

May I be peaceful,

May I be well."

Or make up other similar phrases that particularly resonate with you. Repeat each phrase silently, noticing any reverberations in terms of thoughts, emotions and sensations felt in the body. Noticing any pull of "moving toward," or any resistance or "pushing away." Whatever you notice is simply feedback and an acknowledgment of how things are right now.

CONTINUE FOR AS LONG AS YOU WANT TO.

People often find this quite a difficult practice to do—wishing ourselves well can go against everything we have been taught. However, it is important because **if we cannot be kind to ourselves, how can we hope to be kind to others?**

If you find this practice a struggle, perhaps first try Creating a Circle of Kindness (see pages 128–131), in which we begin by offering kindness to those we care about, and then include ourselves in that circle.

Another way that might make it easier for you, is to do the practice above while holding an image of yourself as a vulnerable child in your mind's eye.

> *Feel free to change the phrases as you wish—although beware of getting sidetracked in searching for the perfect words. Sometimes people find it helpful to add the caveat "… as it is possible for me to be" if the state you are describing feels out of reach at that time.*

THOSE WHO IRRITATE US

We all have people in our life who rub us up the wrong way. I once did the following practice focusing on a colleague I was in daily contact with, but with whom I had a difficult relationship. She was **grumpy, demanding, and often rude** (so I thought), but it was an important relationship for both of us. I could do nothing about her attitude, but I could do something about mine and so for a while **she became my focus** in a Loving Kindness practice, in which **I wished this person well**, picturing her as someone who wanted to be happy, liked, and loved.

As I progressed with this practice, **the difference in our relationship was remarkable.** However, the change was in me; I had done nothing to her. I now saw her in a new light, which changed the way I related to her. It was **not an intellectual change, but an emotional one**. Although we never became friends, we established a good working relationship.

Try this

Sit in a comfortable position and before you start, choose someone who is irritating you. (I strongly recommend that you do not choose anyone who has hurt you significantly—keep it small, manageable, and safe, as this practice can stir up strong emotions.)

Take some time to settle into your posture, connecting with the breath and the body. It is important first to establish a good sense of the breath, so that you can come back to it any time things become difficult.

Bring to mind your chosen person. It can be helpful to picture the person somewhere he or she can't reach you (such as on an island surrounded by shark-infested waters.) Wherever you picture the person, begin wishing him or her well, using the following phrases or others of your own.

"May you be well/happy,

May you be free from anger/hate,

May you be calm/peaceful."

Silently repeating the phrases, feel the resonance ripple out and notice the effect on the body, the mind, and the emotions. Return your attention to the breath if any of these become too strong. (If you feel overwhelmed at any time, return to Offering Kindness to Yourself on pages 132–4 and do this for a while.)

You need to do this **practice regularly.** Doing it once is unlikely to create any change. However, it is better **initially to do it for only a few minutes** sandwiched between longer periods of Mindfulness of Breathing (see pages 44–5) and **gradually build up the time.**

Remember we are not seeking to change the other person's behavior or attitudes in any way. **Any changes will arise in us**, not in them, but the way we interact with them may affect their response to us.

> " Our body is a true barometer of our feelings. I was doing this practice with someone who was causing a lot of hurt to a friend. When I tried to say "May you be well," I was surprised to feel a strong resistance in my body. One part of me was saying "Come on Anna, wish him well…" yet the other flatly refused. There was no way my true self was prepared to do this, even if intellectually I wanted to. Remembering a teaching by Joseph Goldstein, I explored what I would be prepared to wish, testing different phrases against the sensations I felt in my body. After a few moments I came up with "May you be free from anger," since this was the emotion that was driving this person's behavior, and I could feel no resistance in my body to saying this. I continued the practice using just that phrase. "

WISHING WELL

I was first introduced to the idea of combining a traditional Loving Kindness practice with walking by author and meditation teacher Sharon Salzberg. Doing the two practices together transforms the formal Loving Kindness practice to one that is informal, which you can do anywhere.

As with the other practices of this kind, it is important that you **choose phrases that resonate with you**. The ones here are simply suggestions, so please feel free to change them.

Remember, too, that we are not practicing Loving Kindness with a view to changing anyone, we are simply **sending good wishes to ourselves and others.**

Try this

Begin walking. If you are doing this informally, walk at a pace that is normal for you, otherwise you may wish to walk more slowly than usual. While you are walking, repeat the following phrases silently to yourself:

"May I be well,

May I be happy,

May I be free from suffering."

Perhaps pause in between each phrase and let each one drop, settle, and resonate through the body. Every time you get pulled away by thoughts of someone else, or you become aware of another living being around you (and this includes animals and insects), extend your awareness to incorporate them, too:

"May we be well" and so on.

Then, return to saying the phrases just for yourself again.

LETTING GO OF TECHNOLOGY

Our cell phones, smart phones, laptops, and MP3 players are all supposed to **make life better** for us. They enable us to stay in touch with friends and family, and to listen to music we enjoy. However, these gadgets also connect us to the office 24/7, and distract us from what we are doing. How often are you interrupted from what you are doing by the beep of an incoming text, phone call, or email? There is nothing wrong with technology until it interferes with our relationships with others. **What is your relationship with your gadgets?**

Try this

Give yourself the gift of uninterrupted time by making a conscious
decision not to answer phone calls and emails, or to listen to music. If
going cold turkey feels too big a jump, perhaps just decide to focus on
one thing, such as going to work without having headphones on.
Other suggestions are:

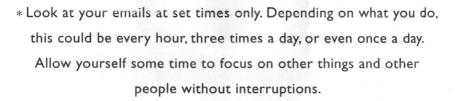

* Look at your emails at set times only. Depending on what you do,
this could be every hour, three times a day, or even once a day.
Allow yourself some time to focus on other things and other
people without interruptions.

* Turn off your phone whenever you can or, at least, put it on silent.

* Avoid bringing phones to meals.

* Avoid taking your phone to any activity that is
supposed to be time off.

* When you are with family, and especially children, give them your
full attention rather than splitting it. You will all benefit.

chapter 5

WEAVING YOUR PARACHUTE

Jon Kabat-Zinn talks of the importance of establishing a mindfulness **practice while life is going well** and you are feeling strong. By doing this you are learning and practicing skills ("weaving your parachute") that **will be invaluable when life throws up obstacles**. It is much harder to try to learn something new when we are in crisis.

The practices in this section are what I call foundational practices. These are the practices I come back to time and time again: watching the breath (see pages 146–7), tuning in to my weather forecast (see pages 163–4), and practicing staying with the itch (see pages 152–3). If you are a creature of habit, deliberately **putting yourself outside your comfort zone** by doing something different (see page 154) **will gently build up your stress tolerance level**.

The more you can exercise your muscle of awareness, the more resilient you will be in times of stress. Research has shown that you can "bank" stress resilience in the body, so **make the most of times when life is going smoothly**—it will pay dividends later when times are tougher.

WAKING UP TO MINDLESSNESS

When we start paying attention to ourselves, the first thing we notice is just how mindless we are. We **become aware of how judgmental we are about others and how these judgments influence our thoughts, actions, and behavior**. We often notice after the event how quick we were to react automatically to someone or something, which may lead us to regret what we have said or done.

We often have a tendency to see these mindless moments as another one of our faults. However, it is far better to **seize them as opportunities for congratulation**. The fact that we are noticing how mindless we are is an important first step—the **noticing is a moment of wakefulness and clear seeing**. Until we see something for what it really is there is no possibility of doing it differently.

So next time you notice a judging thought about someone or something, label it—tell yourself the "judging mind" is present.

When you realize you could have handled someone or something better, congratulate yourself on the act of noticing this, **acknowledge how you might have done things differently**, and remind yourself that the gap between reaction and response will become narrower with practice. For this is a practice—**we have to do it over and over again to learn new habits** and wiser responses. We will forget and we will need to start over. This will always happen and it is integral to the process of practicing.

> *Notice the judging mind or an inappropriate response with a spirit of kindness rather than compounding the response with condemnation. We are all "works in progress."*

THE BREATH

Mindfulness of breathing is one of the first practices people often learn. One reason for this is that the **breath is a great focus for a practice because it is always there**, so by tuning in to it regularly, we are creating an anchor that will help stabilize us when things get difficult.

When we do the breathing meditations we are not trying to change our way of breathing, rather we are just noticing how it is right now. **How we are breathing gives us great feedback on our current state of mind**. Noticing the qualities of our breathing—whether it is short or long, shallow or deep, and so on—can be really useful, as can becoming familiar with how we breathe normally and how the breath changes if we are anxious or angry.

You may notice that the act of **focusing your attention on the breath changes it**. If this happens there is no need to worry. If it feels okay, just continue watching the breath and feeling the physical sensations of breathing.

Sometimes people have strong negative associations with the breath that can cause a breathing meditation to be problematic. If this applies to you, I recommend that you take your attention to your feet on the floor. You can do this as an alternative practice (see pages 188–9) or you can switch between the breath and the feet on the floor, staying with the breath perhaps only for a moment or two before grounding yourself through paying attention to the feet for a longer period. This is a safe way to **practice being with the breath** at a pace and in a way that feels right for you.

When we are watching the breath, the only instruction is to **notice and experience the physical sensations of breathing**: the expansion and contraction of the belly, the rise and fall of the chest. Stay with the length of each in-breath and each out-breath and notice, too, the spaces between— when an out-breath turns into an in-breath, and back again.

The moment you realize you are somewhere else and your mind has been pulled away by thoughts, notice this and come back to the breath. **Let go of any negative thoughts** such as "I'm hopeless at this," or "See—I can't even stay focused on the breath." In fact, these moments of waking up are moments of congratulation. In such moments of realization, you are truly present. All you have to do is come back to the breath and start over again. **This is the practice**.

MINDFULNESS OF BREATHING

This practice is great for getting in to the body and it also develops concentration. It is a good way to **practice tuning in to the breath** and if you do this regularly, **you will find it easier to anchor yourself when things are difficult**. You can do it informally any time and in any place so no one need know you are doing it. You can also do it as a formal sitting practice at home (see pages 38–41 for posture tips). Follow the instructions on pages 44–51.

You can do this for as short or as long a period as you wish. If you are doing it as a longer formal practice, see pages 18–19 for suggestions on managing time.

> *To support your practice it can be helpful to always place your attention on the same part of the body. Choose the area where you feel the breath most strongly—for example, the belly or the chest.*

Counting the Breath

This is another practice for getting into the body, and building focus and attention. Counting the breath can be helpful if you are feeling particularly distracted, as the counting process acts as a scaffold on which to build. You can do this as an informal practice, but it is more commonly done as a formal sitting practice.

Take your seat as described on page 39. Starting on an in-breath, count up to five on subsequent in-breaths. Then start again at one. When (and it will be "when" rather than "if") you find yourself going past five, just go back to one again as soon as you realize.

Your mind will wander and you will keep starting over. This is the practice.

Focusing on the in-breath and/or the out-breath.

A variation on Counting the Breath is to focus on either the in-breath or the out-breath. Choose either one at the start of the practice and keep to this for the entire time rather than switching between the two.

It can be interesting to notice the different qualities the variations cultivate. Play, experiment, and investigate for yourself. Be curious about your breath.

TAKING A BREATHING SPACE

It is a good idea to **have a quick way of shifting gears and coming into the present moment**. This can be done as a mini-meditation throughout your day, but is also especially helpful when things seem difficult in your life. However, **do not use it to try to fix or change an experience**. Your experience may be different after doing this practice but, equally, it may be the same as it was before.

The breathing space is an opportunity to pause and shift from "doing" mode into "being." We notice what is arising for us in terms of thoughts, emotions, and physical sensations and we acknowledge their presence (even if we wish they weren't there.) Then we turn our attention to the breath and breathe with all that is arising. This coming into the present moment is the first step to accepting what is arising.

> *It can be helpful to schedule this mini-meditation into your day, perhaps choosing an event to peg it to, for example, each mealtime. When you forget (which you often will) just do the Breathing Space the moment you remember. Gradually the process of scheduling will help this practice become something you do throughout the day.*

Try this

The Breathing Space was developed by mindfulness teacher and trainer Trish Bartley, and people often say it is the practice they do most regularly. It takes just a couple of minutes and you can do it anywhere, without anyone knowing.

It is helpful to see the Breathing Space as a three-step practice. Start in a posture that reflects an inner attitude of alert attention (sitting, standing, or lying down.)

Step 1 Acknowledge what you are thinking... what emotions are present and what physical sensations you are feeling in the body (if any.) This is a noticing and naming step. We are not analyzing or judging what the experience is, or whether it is appropriate or politically correct. We are simply acknowledging what is there— and there may be nothing and that is just your experience now.

Step 2 Taking your attention to your breath, begin feeling the sensations of breathing. If it is helpful, you can repeat silently to yourself, "breathing in, breathing out." Stay with the breath for a few moments.

Step 3 Widen your focus of attention from the breath to include the whole body, becoming aware of points of contact, such as your feet on the floor or your buttocks on a chair... becoming aware of the room you are in... of any sounds... of any smells... In this state of alert awareness, continue with your day.

STAYING WITH THE ITCH

The formal meditation practices, such as the body scan, sitting or movement practice all provide plenty of opportunities for different states of mind, such as impatience, frustration, boredom, irritation, peacefulness, calmness, and so on, to arise. **Learning to "be with" various states of mind when we practice can help us cope** with them when they arise in everyday life.

Try this

Whatever kind of practice we are doing, we are never deliberately making ourselves uncomfortable and we certainly do not want to sit grimly through pain. However, we can practice not reacting to small discomforts, such as an itch or pins and needles.

We practice "being with" discomfort by turning toward it… becoming interested in how it is really "is"… where it is… what qualities it has… whether it is constant or changing… When we are interested in something, we want to find out more about it. We are curious. This is a very different approach to pushing something away, because we do not like it.

So practice staying with the itch—the literal itch and the metaphorical itch. It could be in a formal sitting practice or something arising in everyday life—perhaps the urge to fidget in an important meeting—but experiment with what it is like to respond to it rather than react to it.

TIP Author and meditation teacher Jack Kornfield suggests the "three-strikes rule." If you notice a desire, say, to scratch an itch or to end a practice, he suggests simply noticing the urge and then letting it go. When it arises again (and it will), let it go again. Then, when it arises a third time, you can give yourself permission to move or "scratch", but do so mindfully—that is, with full awareness of what you are doing while you are doing it.

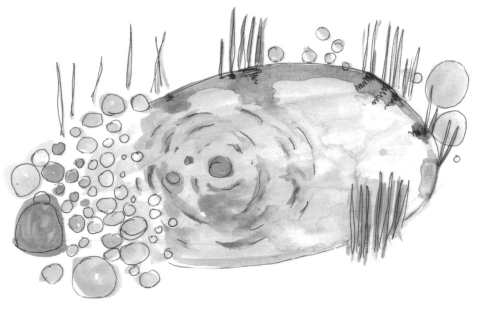

DOING SOMETHING DIFFERENT

Many of us are creatures of habit. **There is a sense of security and comfort in knowing what is going to happen next** and if we are vulnerable to anxiety, we tend to try to control as much of our day as possible. This becomes problematic when life throws up **an obstacle and suddenly we are struggling to remain standing on shifting sands**, which adds additional stress and increases our anxiety.

If we can experiment with extending the boundaries of our comfort zone when things are stable, we will be better able to cope when life goes awry.

Try this

First, take stock of your daily routine. How predictable is your daily routine?

Remember that it is not helpful to make judgments about what you discover. It is just a snapshot of where you are right now.

Now, experiment with doing something in a completely different way. Choose something small, such as what you have for lunch or the route you regularly take to work. Next, decide how long you will do this one thing differently—for example, for one day or one week.

Then, do it! Be creative. Be playful.

HAVE SOME FUN WITH IT AND SEE WHAT YOU NOTICE.

BEFRIENDING THE WANTING CREATURE

A poem by the fifteenth-century Indian mystic, Kabir, begins "I said to the wanting-creature inside me…" When I feel the pull of craving—whether it is for an extra piece of chocolate, a book, or some gadget—I **imagine this little creature inside** me waking up, uncurling, and stretching, and **making itself known**. It has a strongly felt, identifiable presence.

Now I recognize my "wanting-creature" and I try to watch it rather than give in to it. Will it settle back to sleep after a burst of energy or will it hang around? Sometimes, I do feed it and I will have the literal and metaphorical chocolate, but I am taking the chocolate with a sense of knowing what I am doing (and its consequences) rather than taking it and eating it automatically.

We can be pulled into all kinds of cravings—for material goods, particular circumstances, relationships— and identifying and **making friends with your inner wanting-creature may help you make wiser choices**.

Try this

Next time you feel a strong urge to do something, take your attention to the body. What sensations do you feel there? Whereabouts do you feel the sense of wanting most strongly?

Be curious to find out more about your wanting-creature... what it is attracted to... what drives its cravings...

Experiment with what happens if you feed it—how do you feel afterward? What happens if you ignore it? What do you notice if you acknowledge its presence (for example by saying to yourself, "I see you,") but don't act on its demands? Play with the wanting-creature inside you.

As you become familiar with its characteristics you may start noticing its appearance more readily; you may begin to notice the nuances between degrees of wanting. Once you are aware that your choices are being hijacked by its arrival, you are more likely to wrest back control to make your decisions.

" In the beginning it is common to remember after the event that we were trying to notice something. When this happens, use it as an opportunity for practice rather than disappointment. If you are already eating a piece of chocolate taken automatically, begin eating it mindfully, paying attention to the act of eating. Notice what it feels like during eating and notice, too, how the body feels afterward. Become aware of thoughts and emotions arising. You may also notice that once you acquire an object, whatever it is, it becomes less interesting and your attention may move quickly on to something else. Use this as an opportunity to learn and remember, so that next time the wanting-creature throws a tantrum, you can remind yourself of how you felt when you gave in to it. "

WATCHING RESISTANCE

Much of our **unhappiness arises because things are not as we would like them to be**—we want to be thinner, more beautiful, healthier, wealthier, live somewhere less busy or perhaps livelier, change jobs, have a partner, or get divorced… **the list is endless and different** for each of us. We may also experience aversion to the homeless person in the street or the starving child on the television, turning away from them because acknowledging their presence forces us to confront their reality (or our own.) Moreover, **we may feel resistance** to taking exercise even though we know it is good for us; likewise with practicing meditation. In the following exercise, we are not interested in why, but simply in **what it is about our experience that we are resisting**, and noticing how that resistance feels in the body.

Try this

Begin by noticing the moments you habitually resist or turn away from.

Pay attention to the body   particularly to any sense of stiffening up or turning away from someone or something. Notice any tension in the body, identify where it is and what form it takes... maybe noticing a grimace or a facial expression that occurs... an external or internal recoil from something or someone.

As you notice resistance in its multitude of forms, acknowledge its presence. Say to yourself, "Ah, I see you!" or "Resistance (or 'not wanting') is here." Be sure to name it with compassion rather than with judgment. Acknowledge its presence and simply allow it to be there, instead of the more typical response of pushing it away. Perhaps explore it a bit further... finding out what resistance feels like to you. Where do you feel it in the body? (Be as precise as you can about its location.) Identify its shape and feeling tone—is it hard, soft, jagged, or smooth? Is it warm or cold, solid or ethereal? Does it have a color? Does it move around or is it constant?

Be curious about resistance. How do you know you don't like something or someone, or don't want to do something? Remember, we are not trying to change it or make it go away, instead we simply want to learn more about it, so that we can recognize it when it shows up.

We begin to notice the energy that is needed to maintain the resistance. Become aware of the energy required to hold the body tense… How does this make you feel? What could you do differently?

Begin noticing what or who you habitually turn away from—it may be someone at work who you don't get on with or perhaps a neighbor. Whether you are aware of your antipathy or not, it will be coloring your relationship and interactions with that person.

When we become aware what and who we habitually turn away from, we can take account of this and make allowances for our judgmental attitudes, and perhaps deliberately set out to approach them differently, turning toward them instead of away from them. We can also breathe into the area of the body where we feel the aversion, directing the breath, and breathing with the resistance, allowing the breath to come up close to aversion, to "not wanting."

NOTICE WHAT HAPPENS. BE WITH RESISTANCE.

It can feel counterintuitive to pay attention deliberately to the sensations of resistance and aversion that you feel, so always begin with a minor irritation or, if that feels too challenging, perhaps start off with noticing when you are craving or wanting something or someone (see pages 155–7).

SITTING LIKE A MOUNTAIN

In this sitting practice we deliberately cultivate the qualities of a mountain. In *Wherever You Go There You Are*, Jon Kabat-Zinn highlights the important role that mountains play in mythology and religion, and suggests that we can **borrow the strength and steadfastness of the mountain and embody it within us during a sitting practice**.

> Some of us find visualizations more difficult than others. If you are struggling to picture a particular mountain, just notice your struggle and any associated thoughts or judgments, and let them go. Then, just imagine that your body is a mountain and connect with the overall shape and strength of mountains in general.

Try this

Sit either on the floor or in a chair, making sure that the lower part of the body is grounded and connected with the earth or the floor and the upper part of the body is alert and rising upward. (See pages 38–9 for posture.)

Take a few moments to connect with the sensations of breathing. Feel the rising and falling of the chest, staying with the length of each in- and out-breath. Then, expand your awareness outward to gain a sense of the whole body sitting here.

Next, bring to mind a mountain you know, or have seen in a book or on television, or make up an image of a mountain. Allow the mountain to take shape in your imagination—perhaps it has a sharp peak or maybe a soft plateau. Visualize the season on the mountain… its slopes may be covered in forest, snow, or bare rock. Your mountain can take any form you wish.

As you continue sitting with the image of your mountain, begin to bring the mountain into the body—your head becomes the peak, your shoulders the upper slopes, the lower part of the body the lower slopes, connecting with the earth. Sit as your mountain … connected, grounded, yet with the peak rising up into the sky.

Now, become aware of the life of the mountain… the passing seasons… the wind… the rain… the snow… and the sunshine, arising and passing away. Yet through it all, the mountain remains, regardless. Perhaps it becomes a little more weathered, but it is still familiar, still there. The mountain just sits.

WHAT IS YOUR WEATHER FORECAST?

We are all familiar with the idea of a weather barometer as an instrument to predict the state of the weather now and in the immediate future. The following practice was devised by mindfulness teacher Trish Bartley, and in it **we are using our body as a barometer to determine the weather of our moods.** By learning to recognize our own "weather" through **becoming familiar with the different feeling tones arising in the body,** we gain feedback about what is going on for us in a particular moment. As we become more practiced at doing this, we can use the body as our own emotional barometer and we can begin to **pick up early signs of particular moods as they arise** and so will be in a better position to take informed action.

Try this

Identify the part of the body where you usually feel stress—this is most commonly in the torso, but try to be as specific as possible in terms of location. You might want to note this down somewhere. Practice tuning in to this part of the body whenever you are feeling stressed, anxious, worried, or experiencing another difficult emotion—be really curious and notice what these states of mind feel like physically.

Then do the same thing when you are feeling positive emotions, such as excitement, happiness, calm, or peacefulness.

Often we are unaware that a particular emotion is influencing and affecting our words and actions. But learning to recognize the feeling "tones" and the constantly shifting patterns of both the positive and negative mind states helps us realize what may be driving our thoughts, words, and actions, and that they constantly change.

HEARING SOUND AND SILENCE

Mindfulness practice is often an exploration of the senses but hearing or sound practice is often overlooked. Usually **when we hear a sound we allocate a meaning to it**, often with an associated story based on our experiences of that sound. Thus if you have been in an accident with emergency vehicles attending every time you hear a siren your body may respond to it as a threat, and all the memories, thoughts, and associations from that time may come to the fore. You may repeatedly relive the event purely because the sound has activated the body memory.

In this practice we are experimenting with **being with sound simply as sound**—a note or notes strung together. When we get pulled away by an associated story, at the moment of noticing this, we let it go and bring our attention back to the sound.

Try this

Take your seat and allow the body to settle, perhaps connecting to the breath for a few minutes to anchor yourself in the body.

Then, imagine your body as a receiver, opening up to sound. These may be far away sounds or internal sounds in the body... hearing... receiving... noticing the effects of different sounds on the body. How does the body react to sound? Just noticing without judgment.

We are not looking for sound—we are not actively "listening". We are simply allowing ourselves to open and receive whatever sound might come into our vicinity, like a radar. Noticing it arising, noticing it passing. Noticing its tone, pitch, timbre. Becoming aware of pure sound.

Noticing the pauses between sounds. The sound of silence.

SITTING BY THE WATERFALL

Our **thoughts are very powerful**. They weave works of fiction that can sweep us into another world. The following sitting practice offers a way of **being with our thoughts**, without letting ourselves be carried away by them.

Try this

Take the time to settle into your seat. Make sure you feel grounded through the floor and/or chair. Connect to the place where you feel the breath most strongly and make that your point of focus. Spend several minutes watching the breath, noticing its effect on the mind and the body.

The breath is your anchor and any time you feel yourself getting swept away by thoughts, use the breath to reel yourself back into the body. You may do this repeatedly.

Picture yourself at the top of a waterfall, sitting safely on a rock, with a sense of the earth beneath, supporting you. Perhaps there are rocks, trees, or bushes you can hold on to. The water is rushing by and cascading over the top, carrying your thoughts, twisting and turning in mini whirlpools…

If you would like to, you can consciously place your thoughts in the water, perhaps launching them out into the current on leaves like rafts. Some thoughts might get stuck behind a rock and remain in sight, but the power of the water soon pushes them on.

As you sit on the rock, you may be soaked by the water spray but you are not getting swept away. Your thoughts pass by, tumbling over the edge, out of sight and out of mind. You remain sitting, watching them.

PAYING ATTENTION

In *A Heart as Wide as the World*, Sharon Salzberg tells a lovely story about being on a retreat. Sharon went for an interview with her teacher, U Pandita, expecting to relate her meditation experience but instead he asked her to tell him everything about putting on her shoes. She had not paid any attention to putting on her shoes so she went away and noticed all that was involved in putting on her shoes. She returned for her next interview confident that she could tell all. However, her teacher was no longer interested in shoes but asked her what she had noticed about washing her face; having been so focused on noticing the thoughts, feelings, and sensations around "putting on shoes", Sharon had noticed nothing about washing her face. As each day passed, not knowing what her teacher would ask her next, Sharon started to pay attention to every experience of her day.

Try This

Imagine you have been asked to tell someone everything there is to know about how you put on your shoes. Notice what you do and what it feels like. Then choose something else, such as:

* Putting on your clothes

* Shaving

* Putting on your make-up

* Eating breakfast

* Taking a shower

* Cleaning your teeth

* Leaving the house

* Going to work

* Dressing a child

* Changing a baby

The beauty is that you don't have to do anything differently in order to practice. Simply be aware of what it is you usually do and that is the practice. Notice as much about your experience as you can in terms of what you feel physically in the body, what you feel emotionally, what thoughts are present, and how your intentions affect your actions.

THE POWER OF SILENCE

The power of silence has always been recognized but it has never been needed more than today. **Our world is noisier than ever**—we have headphones permanently attached to our ears and we incessantly interact with the world through emails, the Internet, and phones. Although these technologies have their benefits, **they can also serve as distractions and give us ways to just avoid being with ourselves**. Staying silent and setting aside the distraction of reading and interacting with others can be liberating. We are **freed from the need to make conversation or to assume a particular personality**, and silence allows us to **notice more acutely both what is happening internally and in the world around us**. Our senses are heightened and our experience is **sharper, richer, and more intense**.

Try This

Dropping into silence can feel daunting and, unless you go away on retreat, it can be impractical to arrange at home. However, it is possible to be silent while doing a short activity, such as eating a meal or going out for a walk. You can deliberately switch off any gadgets, such as your computer, cell phone, or MP3 player. Experiment by starting with a short period that feels manageable and extend it when you can.

THE GUIDELINES FOR SILENCE VARY BUT GENERALLY THEY ARE:

* No speaking (although if you come across someone else who is not aware that you are remaining silent, it is fine to exchange necessary words.)

* No reading; no listening to music/radio; no watching television.

* Sometimes no eye contact is suggested, too—although this can bring up strong feelings in people. No eye contact strips away another way of communicating.

* Writing is sometimes discouraged but silence can also open up a well of creativity, so it is a personal choice.

While in silence, it is fine to continue with routine activities, such as cooking, cleaning, gardening, walking, and so on. You can, of course, do formal meditation practices as well. **When we are in silence, everything we do is part of one seamless practice**.

Dropping into silence is an opportunity to experience how our "weather" changes from one moment to the next. When we are silent, **we notice how desperately we crave stimulation** as we become engrossed in, say, reading instructions on how to turn on a fire extinguisher or the label on the jam jar. **We might do everything more slowly**, as we are no longer rushing on to the next thing; or we might experience a burst of restlessness as the stillness grates. **We notice** the colors on our plate and subtle flavors we usually miss, and our sense of smell is heightened, so we take more care about what we are eating. **We become aware** of the junk that fills our mind, the thoughts that circle us hour after hour.

Being in silence for several hours is not always easy or enjoyable but it is always invaluable.

When coming out of a longer period of silence, such as a day or more, take care to **ease yourself back into the noise of everyday life**. Be careful when doing any activity in which your safety depends on your reflexes, such as driving, as these may be slower than usual at first.

chapter 6

BEING WITH THE DIFFICULT

Mindfulness can help us deal with difficult emotions more easily than we might do otherwise. However, **before we jump into trying to solve all our problems with mindfulness, it is important to have established some basic skills**, such as regularly returning to the breath (see pages 146–9) and tuning in to the body (see chapter 2).

The purpose of the practice is not to fix or make things better, but to practice being with or perhaps simply turning toward difficult sensations, emotions, and thoughts. When we become aware of what is going on in the body and we have a willingness to experience unpleasant sensations, we may notice them changing and they may go away, but they may not. However, **the very act of being curious about your experience immediately shifts you into the stance of an observer**, which means you are less caught up in the emotion.

It is important to take small steps to prevent yourself feeling overwhelmed by feelings and sensations. Practice on the small, irritating things in life. **Sometimes the wisest action is to do nothing**, and instead wait for a time and a place in which you will feel safe to practice.

Remember that the breath is always your anchor, your place of safety, and if you don't feel comfortable focusing on the breath, you can always take your focus to the feet on the floor instead (see pages 188–9).

SITTING AND MOVING WITH THE BREATH

Mindfulness of breathing is one of the core practices and I recommend you practice doing it informally, see pages 150–1, as well as sometimes doing slightly longer more formal sitting practices, see pages 44–5 and 146–9.

When we are feeling anxious. it can be challenging to sit still. Our mind is all over the place with our thoughts racing here, there, and everywhere. If sitting still feels too much, **an option is to incorporate some movement into your sitting.** You could either do this for a few minutes at the start of the practice and then, **if you start feeling settled, just stop,** or you can do it for the entire time.

The practice is the same as Mindfulness of Breathing (see pages 44–5), but we are going to **introduce a small movement of the hands.** This is a variation of a standing exercise done in Qiqong (pronounced "chi-gung") and if you like movement practices, **I recommend finding out more about Qiqong.**

Before starting you may find it helpful to review the instructions about the breath on pages 44–5.

Try this

Sit in a comfortable posture (see pages 38–41) with your hands in your lap, palms up. Your eyes can be open or closed.

Take your attention to the part of the body where you feel the breath most strongly—it could be the belly, the chest, or around the nostrils and lips. Begin by noticing the breath—becoming aware of your breath right now... noticing its qualities and characteristics, but not worrying about having to change it.

As you breathe in, let your hands float upward, palms up, for the length of the in-breath... As you breathe out, turn the hands over, palms down, letting them float back down to your lap.

Continue doing this, moving the hands in time with the breath, breathing in... hands floating up; breathing out... hands floating down.

Whenever you notice your mind being pulled away by thoughts (which will happen), come back to the breath, picking up the movement of the hands.

REMEMBER THROUGHOUT TO CULTIVATE A SENSE OF KINDNESS AND COMPASSION TOWARD YOURSELF AND WHAT YOU ARE DOING.

RED MEANS STOP

How many times have you driven up to traffic lights as they changed from green to amber to red and felt your emotions begin to rise? **When the lights are against us, it can feel as if the whole world is against us, too**—especially if there is somewhere we want or need to be. We take it personally: "The light saw me coming and changed to red… deliberately." Does that sound familiar?

When we feel like this, we get irritated and possibly angry. **Perhaps there is a recurring story about "this always happens to me"** or something similar. We may tighten our grip on the steering wheel, our palms might begin to sweat, perhaps we drum our fingers in the hope of speeding things up a little… we may start muttering to ourselves or perhaps snapping at others in the car. We might pull out to do a quick lane change in the hope of gaining a second or two when the lights go to green…

But however we respond, if we want to keep our license we have to **stop at a red light**. **No ifs, no buts**, that's the way it is all over the world. Getting irritated and tense at something we can do nothing about has consequences:

The red light can be a signal to stop and pay attention to our experience

* Our fight-or-flight mechanism is kept on high alert with a detrimental effect on our health (see pages 20–24).

* It has a negative effect on our emotions.

* Our mood affects how we interact with others as well as how we interpret events.

* What if there was an alternative? What if we could see the red light as an opportunity rather than an obstacle?

Try This

As the light changes from amber to red and you come to a stop, notice what is happening to you… Paying attention to your experience, noticing…

What thoughts arise?

What emotions can you feel?

What physical sensations are present? Noticing any felt sensations arising in the body, particularly points of contact with the steering wheel… How are your shoulders? Your neck?

REMEMBER…

We are not trying to change our experience but rather just noticing what it is and what is happening to it, moment by moment. **Often sensations might be subtle.** You may not feel or notice anything and that is okay. Making the intention of turning toward it is what is important. Whenever your mind gets pulled away by thoughts, **just keep coming back to the body**; perhaps noticing the rising and falling of the breath, the expansion and contraction of the chest, feeling the weight of the feet on the floor, your hands on the wheel, your body in the seat… **Just sitting**.

Reminding yourself that in this moment there is nowhere else to go… **Just being present**. Practice as long as the light remains red.

Afterward, **reflect on what you noticed**.

COMMUTING CHALLENGES

I was **sitting on the bus in the sweltering heat**—my discomfort exacerbated by **heavy bags on my lap**. A rather corpulent gentleman got on and took the empty seat next to me. Although he spilled over on to "my side," we had space between us until the bus filled up and he was forced to edge over to make room for those standing in the aisle. Suddenly he was squashed against me, hot and sticky, **and automatically I tutted**. As I felt his recoil we both started apologizing simultaneously. I knew it was not his fault. My discomfort was as much due to the weight of my bags and the sun beating through the window. I

If we can change the way

explained this to him and apologized and within seconds we were chatting about the unpleasantness of the heat.

In this situation I was already uncomfortable and **my fellow passenger was simply the proverbial last straw**. My "tut" of displeasure was done without thinking, but as it occurred I was aware of his embarrassment as well as the wider picture of the bags (my fault) and the heat (no one's fault.) **I could do nothing about my automatic reaction, but I could choose my next response**—my apology and explanation. Neither made up for the potential hurt I caused him, but I hope they went some way to alleviating it.

If you commute on public transport, you will know how **frequently you find yourself in testing situations with fellow travelers**. Too often, we arrive for work frazzled and grumpy because of interactions such as this. But what if we could do something different –**what if we could turn the commute into an opportunity for practice?**

we relate to an experience, it may cease being stressful to us.

Try these

The next time you are feeling fraught when you commute, try doing one of the following practices:

1. Take your attention into the body, becoming aware of its response. What are you reacting against? Notice any sense of tightening, contracting, or pulling away. As you become aware of your experience, you can choose how you respond. You can take your attention to the area of tightness and explore it further. You can also take your attention to the breath and use the breath as an anchor, staying with the length of each in-breath and each out-breath. Alternatively, you can direct the breath into the part of the body that feels tense, breathing in and out through that specific area.

2. We often have a set idea of how something should pan out and when someone interferes with that scenario we are disappointed. This then ripples out into other interactions. Instead, if we can remain open about possible outcomes, we are less likely to have particular expectations. For example, if you expect to get a seat on a bus or a train and then you find they are all taken, you will feel deprived. But if you can let go of any expectations of getting a seat and simply remain open to the possibility of one being available, finding or being offered a seat becomes a bonus. Letting go of expectations can open up opportunities—you may see something interesting, or read a job advertisement over someone's shoulder...
the possibilities are endless.

3. It is usual to feel more stressed when our choices are taken away from us. Using the seat scenario above, if we make a beeline for an empty seat and someone cuts in and takes it, we usually feel annoyed (like when someone steals an empty parking space in front of you.) However, I have found that if I make a deliberate choice to stop and bow out of the "competition," and offer the seat to the other person, I don't feel hard done by. I may still be standing, but I'm not standing with a cloud of irritation hanging over me. If I can perceive the situation in another way and become indifferent to getting a seat, the situation will no longer trigger my body's stress reaction because it is not seen as taxing.

4. Many of us feel excessively time-pressured—we need to get into the office by a certain time and if we don't, it will be a "disaster." We have to get this train rather than wait two minutes for the next one, because otherwise we'll be late. So, we wait anxiously, not sure if there will be room. The doors open and we join the throng pushing forward to make room for "just one more." We cram ourselves in and arrive at work stressed. But what if you let that train go and wait for the next one, or even the one after it? If you arrive six minutes later, but in a much calmer state, is that not a better start to the day? It's your choice.

BUMPER TO BUMPER

The beauty of mindfulness meditation is that **life always presents us with plenty of opportunities to practice.** This is another practice to do in the car in a traffic jam. It is likely to be a longer practice than that on pages 178–81, but it is a similar process.

This practice can be done anywhere you have to wait—for example, at the supermarket check-out, at the bank, and so on. Make an intention to **transform every line from an obstacle into an opportunity to practice mindfulness**. By practicing "being with" the small irritations of everyday life, we are practicing turning toward and being curious about experiences that are perhaps stressful, but that are not going to overwhelm us.

Try this

Begin by making an intention to be present in your experience, however much you wish it were different.

Explore turning toward the experience—first noticing any thoughts that might be arising, noting them as thoughts... Then, become aware of any emotions, perhaps naming them to yourself (see pages 190–1)—for example, "Anger is here," and acknowledging their presence, even if you feel they are inappropriate. If you notice judgments arising around the emotions, just note: "judging."

And then turn your attention to your body. What are you noticing here? Become interested in the body's response to the experience. What sensations are you feeling? How would you describe them? Where are the sensations located? Are they fixed or moving around?

Continue exploring the experience, becoming interested in it. While you are stuck here in your car, there is nothing else to do but find out a bit more about it...

Afterward, reflect back on what you noticed while practicing mindfulness in the traffic jam.

STAYING GROUNDED

When things are feeling difficult, it is easy to become overwhelmed with emotions. **Our thoughts can quickly catastrophize us into a state of anxiety.** The usual recommendation when things get difficult is to go to the breath, but for some people and on some occasions, this can be hard to do. **If we are panicking our breathing is often affected** and the idea of turning our attention to it seems too **much to ask. The alternative is simple and can also take you into the body** (which is the reason we focus on the breath.)

You can do this practice anywhere and no one need know you are doing it.

Try this

Whether you are standing or sitting down, take your attention to your feet and become aware of them on the floor. Note the sensations of the feet making contact with the floor, perhaps noticing touch, warmth, coolness… Become aware of the feet touching the floor.

Every time your thoughts pull you away into the past or the future, just escort your attention back to the feet. You can do this over and over again.

After a few minutes, if you would like to, expand your awareness out from the feet to include the breath. As you breathe in, imagine you are breathing in through the feet… filling the body with air… filling the body with oxygen… and then breathing out through the feet, letting the air go.

Continue doing this, breathing in deeply through the feet… breathing out through the feet… as long as you wish to, bringing your attention back to the feet whenever it wanders.

NAMING YOUR DEMONS

Traditional Buddhist practices include naming any emotions that may arise while practicing, for example, saying silently, "Jealousy is here" or whatever it is that you identify. **Naming the emotion in this way objectifies it and the namer becomes an observer with the perspective that that entails**, rather than "being jealous," which suggests being caught up in that emotion. Research has also shown that the act of naming an emotion activates a part of the brain involved in self-regulation. **The bare fact of naming is what is important**, rather than any subsequent conclusions you may draw about that emotion. So when we name what is arising, we are actively dampening down that emotion—as well as taking the observer stance.

The following practice is usually done as part of a sitting practice, but you could also do it informally in your everyday life when you notice difficult emotions arising.

Try this

Whenever you notice a strong emotion arising, identify it and note it—for example, say "Sadness is here" or softly repeat "Sadness, sadness, sadness." At the same time notice what "sadness" feels like in the body. Sometimes there may be more than one emotion arising—for example, anger may be the first, strongest emotion, but fear is often found underlying it. So, sometimes it can be helpful to just sit and notice how emotions wax and wane. You may be surprised when you identify what comes up.

As always, it is important to remember with all of these practices that we are not doing them to make them disappear. This is one of the paradoxes of meditation—if you practice with the intention of making a difficult emotion go away, you will most likely be disappointed. **We are practicing "being with" whatever arises**.

BEFRIENDING THE DIFFICULT

If we suffer from a chronic illness or condition, we can have a tendency to identify strongly with it—for example, we might say to ourselves: "I am an anxious person." This feels very solid, concrete, and permanent. It sounds as if this is how we are all the time, whereas of course the reality is often very different. Anxiety or pain can come and go with long periods of absence. **The condition is something that appears from time to time like an unwanted friend or relative.** We can **encourage this attitude of distancing ourselves from the condition** by giving it a name—preferably something humorous.

A friend of mine, Elise, was diagnosed in her thirties with rheumatoid arthritis, a painful condition that can be very debilitating at times. Elise calls her condition "Mr Arthur Itis." So she might say, "Arthur turned up at the weekend—absolute pain. I couldn't go out…" Immediately, there is some distance between her and the condition. She does not want it and she cannot stop it arriving out of the blue, but she can stop it defining her. It is only one part of her.

Ask "Can I stay with this for just one breath?"

Try this

If you suffer from an illness, a condition, or a phobia, give it a name.
For example, for fear, anxiety, or pain, you could use
"Mr Fear" or "Annie Anxious," or "Percy Pain." Whatever name you choose, use it
whenever the problem arises. It won't make the problem disappear, but it might
change the way you relate to it.

... Then stay with it for just one more

JUST ONE BREATH

Whether we are in physical or emotional pain, the idea of being able to bear it for any length of time can seem insupportable. **With mindfulness, we are constantly "working the edge" of being with the difficult.**

"Working the edge" is the difference between forcing yourself with gritted teeth to put up with something, which often has a feeling of resistance and tension, and dipping your toe in the water, testing your boundaries and limits. You can **experiment with identifying this difference in a range of scenarios**. I often have a mental image of myself inside a giant plastic bubble that expands toward and into the difficulty, but then withdraws and contracts, while all the time I remain safe and protected inside.

Much of our suffering, whether physical or psychological, is caused by thoughts of having to put up with it for an indeterminate amount of time. We use catastrophizing language, such as "This is killing me," and "I can't put up with this much longer."

However, Jon Kabat-Zinn suggests reframing your approach and asking yourself, "Can I stay with this for just one breath?" After all, the pain is there and you cannot escape it... then, assuming you are coping, staying with it for just one more breath... and so on.

The only instruction is to **stay with one breath at any one time**. Stay with the length of an in-breath, and notice the transition where an in-breath becomes an out-breath, then stay with the length of that out-breath. **There is no expectation of staying with more than that.**

Any time your thoughts pull you away (and they probably will), just come back to the "edge" and **open to the possibility of staying with it** for just one breath more.

A WALK IN THE RAIN

Rain—it is often cold and it is always wet. **How do you usually react to going out in the rain?** Most of us put on a raincoat, possibly gumboots, unfurl the umbrella, and tentatively venture out, head down bracing ourselves literally and metaphorically against the elements…

Next time it rains, why not try something different?

Try this

Allowing the raindrops to bounce off your face, soaking your hair and trickling down your back   Noticing the body's reaction …perhaps a shrinking away or a delight in its coolness… becoming aware of any thoughts or emotions arising…

acknowledging their presence but bringing the attention back to the body. Doing this over and over … Noticing any tensing of muscles… locating tightness and acknowledging it…

Feeling the sensation of water touching skin… tasting raindrops on your tongue… opening to the smell of water and wetness everywhere. Becoming aware of temperature… noticing any sense of being pulled into the experience or wanting to push it away (and remembering we are not seeking a particular outcome).

BE IN THE RAIN…
HOWEVER THAT MAY BE

OPENING TO THE WIDER WORLD

When we are caught up in difficulty, our world becomes small and contracted as we focus totally on our problems. Our thinking also contracts, and **suffering chronic stress has a negative impact on the brain**, preventing new neurons growing and actually causing areas of the brain to atrophy and die. When we are stressed, **we are unlikely to be creative or open to new ideas or ways of thinking**, and we may feel overwhelmed. Connecting to a sense of a wider world can help **counteract this feeling and create a small shift that is enough to set a new tangent**, a change of direction.

Try this

If you are feeling overwhelmed, find a place outside where you can connect with some space. If you are in an urban environment, perhaps try to go somewhere high so you can rise above the crowded streets, or find a patch of green in a park. Or perhaps just look out of a window. If you are in the country or by the sea, you may be able to find a wide-open space with a vista over land or sea.

Whether you are contemplating the water, the land, or the sky, just sit quietly, and "open" to that sense of spaciousness.

Connecting to a sense of timelessness: This mountain that has survived millennia… or this vista that has witnessed the small sorrows and joys of generations of people before me… or these waves that have rolled on shore after shore, connecting families from one side of the world to the another… or even this sky that is eternally blue despite being obscured by clouds or rain from time to time.

JUST SIT, LOOK, AND RECEIVE.

MOVING IN CLOSER TO PAIN

When I have a migraine, the pain is excruciating—there is always a point when it suddenly tips into becoming unbearable and my only recourse is to lie down in the dark. However, I have noticed that **if I pay attention to the pain, there is a softening and loosening** sensation in my forehead and temples. The pain is still there, but the muscles in my face relax their grip and the release of tension is noticeable. When I pay attention to the pain, I can begin to disentangle the sensations. **The process is akin to unraveling a densely knotted skein of embroidery threads, gradually beginning to distinguish specific colors as the loosening creates some space between the knots.** I can pick out the different rhythms and locations of my discomfort. I begin to watch the pain rather than being enveloped in it. It is like surfing a wave rather than being pulled under by it.

Try this

Being with pain is challenging and so it's a good idea to make the most of any opportunity to practice with small episodes, such as a headache, a stubbed toe, or a stomachache.

Take your attention to the location of the pain. Notice what is happening. Although we are not deliberately setting out to relax the area around the pain, very often the act of focusing our attention on it causes a change to occur.

Experiment with moving a bit closer to the discomfort. What do you notice? You can retreat to the anchor of the breath at any time you need to. There is no endurance prize.

Notice any thoughts circling the mind. Are you aware of any particular emotions? What stories are you telling yourself about the experience? Are you adding emotional pain to the physical pain? Are your thoughts helpful or not? You can break the cycle of rumination by taking your attention to the body—this can be to the pain itself (investigating it in terms of location, characteristics, color, temperature, and so on), to the breath, or to physical sensations, such as contact with the surface you are sitting or lying on. Alternatively, you can create a cocktail of all three, moving up closer and then retreating to a place of safety at a pace that feels manageable.

It is important not to expect the pain to just disappear because you pay attention to it. It won't, but paying attention is the opposite of avoidance, so it is the first step in acceptance. It is only through acceptance that we can change our relationship with pain.

BEING WITH THE UNPLEASANT

Mindfulness practice is about turning our attention to whatever comes up—including the unpleasant—even though this may feel counterintuitive. However, **we cannot expect to suddenly just be able to put up with difficult feelings**—it is not about gritting our teeth and bearing whatever may happen. Instead, **we are taking a stance of curiosity and interest, and exploring in order to find out more about what "difficult" means for us.** And we do this by beginning with the small stuff, the minor irritations, and unpleasant experiences that we all face in everyday life.

Try this

Make an intention to become aware of any unpleasant events that come up for you today. This is about noticing the little things: how it feels when someone pushes in front of you in the line or someone takes the last loaf of bread in the store, just before you reach it…

Notice what it is that you are labeling "unpleasant." How do you know it is unpleasant for you? What do you feel in the body and where? What thoughts do you notice arising? What emotions are present—there may be more than one?

Be curious about what pushes your buttons and notice the effect on you: on your body, your thoughts, and your mood. Notice, too, how it affects what comes next. How do you interact with others after this event?

As always, we are doing this with a spirit of compassion and kindness toward ourselves. We all react to unpleasant experiences and this practice is about using such experiences as opportunities to get closer to something that feels difficult and finding out more about it. By practicing with the small stuff we are getting used to turning toward the unpleasant—we are exercising our muscle of awareness with particular regard to the difficult. This will stand us in good stead whenever we are faced with bigger difficulties, such as illness, job loss, and bereavement.

It can be helpful to reflect back at the end of the day and notice perhaps two or three "unpleasant" events, recording what you felt physically in the body, what thoughts and emotions you noticed, as well as how you now feel, looking back. Is there anything about this reflection that surprises you? You can do this practice for several days in a row and then perhaps repeat it every few months. You might also like to try the companion practice, Being With the Good, on pages 105–6.

WHERE TO GO NEXT

If you have found the practices in this book helpful, you may want to consider developing your practice through further reading and perhaps attending a course or joining a sitting group. Always practicing on your own in isolation is challenging.

If you wish to establish a daily practice, a course is the best way to do this. There is much to be gained from sharing your experience and learning with others, and the guidance of a teacher can be particularly helpful. If you want to look for groups local to you, search for MBSR (Mindfulness-Based Stress Reduction), MBCT (Mindfulness-Based Cognitive Therapy) and/or Vipassana or insight meditation. The first two are secular, the third is part of the Buddhist tradition—sitting groups are often linked to a specific Buddhist order.

There are many books about mindfulness meditation techniques, mindfulness for specific groups, such as cancer, anxiety, eating disorders, and so on, as well as different forms of Buddhist meditation. I have listed a few specific titles on page 207, but many of these authors have produced other great books, too. I have also listed some authors you might like to explore. Many authors produce audio books, which often include guided meditations, and these can be particularly helpful.

USEFUL WEBSITES

UK

www.bangor.ac.uk/mindfulness Centre for Mindfulness Research and Practice, Bangor, North Wales. Buy CDs, learn more about mindfulness professional training and classes in North Wales.

www.bemindful.co.uk Learn more about mindfulness and find a course in the UK.

www.gaiahouse.co.uk Gaia House is a retreat centre offering courses and meditation retreats in the Buddhist tradition.

www.londoninsight.org London Insight offers a programme of events based on the insight (Vipassana) meditation tradition.

www.mbct.co.uk Find out more about MBCT and the Oxford Mindfulness Centre.

USA

www.dharma.org Insight Meditation Society, Barre, Massachusetts.

www.mindfulnesstapes.com The website of Jon Kabat-Zinn, selling books and CDs.

www.qigonginstitute.org/main_page/main_page.php Promotes Qigong and Energy Medicine through research and education.

www.soundstrue.com Audio and video titles and downloads.

www.spiritrock.org Spirit Rock Meditation Center is dedicated to the teachings of the Buddha as presented in the Vipassana tradition.

www.umassmed.edu/cfm/home/index.aspx Center for Mindfulness in Medicine, Health Care, and Society, University of Massachusetts. Professional training and MBSR programs.

BOOKS

Burch, Vidyamala *Living Well with Pain and Illness: The Mindful Way to Free Yourself from Suffering* (Piatkus, 2008)

Kabat-Zinn, Jon *Full Catastrophe Living: Using the Wisdom of Your Body and Mind to Face Stress, Pain, and Illness* (Delta, 1990)

Kabat-Zinn, Jon *Wherever You Go, There You Are: Mindfulness Meditation in Everyday Life* (Hyperion, 2005)

Kabat-Zinn, Jon and Myla *Everyday Blessings: The Inner Work of Mindful Parenting* (Hyperion, 1998)

Kabat-Zinn, Jon; Teasdale, John; Segal, Zindel; and Williams, Mark *The Mindful Way Through Depression: Freeing Yourself from Chronic Unhappiness* (The Guilford Press, 2007)

Kornfield, Jack *A Path with Heart* (Rider, 2002), plus other titles

Penman, Danny and Williams, Mark *Mindfulness: A Practical Guide to Finding Peace in a Frantic World* (Piatkus, 2011)

I also recommend any books by Pema Chodron, Joseph Goldstein, Thich Nhat Hahn, and Sharon Salzberg. There are many other good book books and authors out there and reading one book will often guide you to another author, so explore your local library and online, too.

ACKNOWLEDGMENTS

Everything I have learned about mindfulness has come from teachers—some face to face and others through their books and audio teachings—as well as from my students and my fellow mindfulness teachers, especially Catherine Grey, who as friend and co-teacher taught and supported me so much.

I owe particular thanks to the teachers on the Masters program at the Centre for Mindfulness Research and Practice in North Wales: Trish Bartley, Becca Crane, David Elias, and Jody Mardula, and especially Eluned Gold for her support and advice as my supervisor, as well as to the teachers from the Center for Mindfulness in Massachusetts, USA, particularly Melissa Blacker and Pamela Erdmann, and David Rynick from Boundless Way Zen.

I would also like to thank London Insight and the regular stream of wonderful teachers there.

Thank you to the team at Cico Books, in particular to Dawn Bates, Sally Powell, Cindy Richards, and Gordana Simakovic for giving me this opportunity, and to Amy Louise Evans for her illustrations.

I give special thanks to Scott and my family for always being there for me, and to Elise Dillsworth for allowing me to share her story.